REVIEWS FOR NICOLA PIERCE

Titanic: True Stories of Her Passengers, Crew and Legacy
'A delightful book and a valuable resource in the *Titanic* canon' *RTÉ.ie*

'Everything by the master historical storytelling Nicola Pierce is sublime'
Writer and art historian Anne Louise Avery

Spirit of the Titanic
'Gripping, exciting and unimaginably shattering' *The Guardian*

Chasing Ghosts
'A fascinating story about Arctic exploration, full of historical detail and
interesting characters. Perfect for readers with adventure in their hearts'
Irish Independent

'There are two stories to *Chasing Ghosts* … equally vivid and gripping. Pierce has
a gift for putting readers at the heart of important moments in history'
Books for Keeps

Kings of the Boyne
'The research into the Battle of the Boyne seeps through with unfading accuracy.
The writing is utterly superb. Though it was over 300 years ago the reader is there.
An incredible reading experience' *Fallen Star Stories*

Behind the Walls
'History as it really happened with its gritty depiction of the terror-struck city of
Derry in 1689 … a vivid evocation of life in a city under siege '
parentsintouch.co.uk

City of Fate
'Will hook you from the start ... historical fiction at its best' *The Guardian*

'A compelling novel ' Robert Dunbar, *Irish Times*

NICOLA PIERCE published her first novel, *Spirit of the Titanic*, to rave reviews. She went on to bring her knowledge of this great ship, and all who sailed in her, to a non-fiction work: *Titanic: True Stories of Her Passengers, Crew and Legacy*. *City of Fate*, her second novel, transported the reader deep into the Russian city of Stalingrad during the Second World War. *Behind the Walls*, a rich emotional novel set in the besieged city of Derry in 1689, was followed with a companion novel, *Kings of the Boyne*, also set in the seventeenth century during a defining moment in Irish history. Nicola then delved deep into the story of explorer Francis Crozier and the Sir John Franklin Arctic North West Passage expedition with two intertwining stories based on real events in nineteenth-century Ireland and the Canadian Arctic in her haunting novel *Chasing Ghosts*.

To read more about Nicola, go to her web page, www.nicolapiercewriter.com.

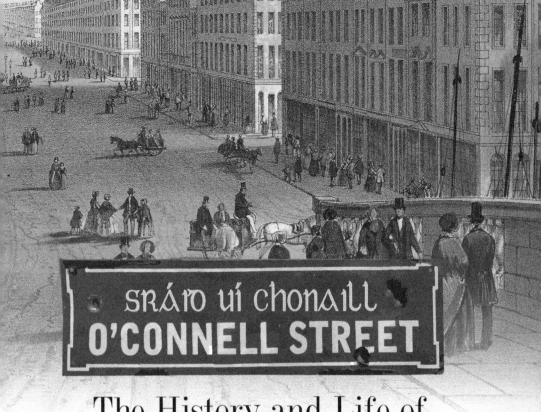

The History and Life of
Dublin's Iconic Street

Nicola Pierce

THE O'BRIEN PRESS
DUBLIN

First published 2021 by The O'Brien Press Ltd,
12 Terenure Road East, Rathgar, Dublin 6, D06 HD27, Ireland.
Tel: +353 1 4923333; Fax: +353 1 4922777
E-mail: books@obrien.ie;
Website: www.obrien.ie
The O'Brien Press is a member of Publishing Ireland.

ISBN: 978–1-78849-148-8

1 3 5 7 9 10 8 6 4 2
21 23 25 24 22

Layout and design by Emma Byrne.
Front cover: O'Connell Street sign inspired by a concept from signsfromireland.com
Cover images: Courtesy of The National Library of Ireland

Printed and bound in Drukarnia Skleniarz, Poland.
The paper in this book is produced using pulp from managed forests.

Published in:

DUBLIN
UNESCO
City of Literature

Dedication

Most of this book was written in lockdown and, because I live in Drogheda, I have not stood on O'Connell Street since March 2020. My last author event was in Eason's just before the schools closed. Would this be a different book without Covid-19? However, a new year brought renewed hope and vaccines.

I would like to dedicate this book to those we lost and to those who fought to keep us safe.

Acknowledgements

This was one of those 'middle of the nights' ideas and I firstly want to thank The O'Brien Press for allowing me bring it to fruition.

I'm neither a historian nor researcher and, therefore, relied on the expertise of others in certain matters. I am particularly grateful to James and Lillie Connolly's grandson Seán Connolly, historian Ronan Fitzpatrick, writer and curator of the An Post Museum Stephen Ferguson, biographer and researcher Eleanor Fitzsimons, Graham Hickey from the Dublin Civic Trust, Peter McDowell from McDowell's Happy Ring House, writer and historian Sinéad McCoole and editor Rachel Pierce for helping me with my various enquiries. Thanks also to Naomi Ní Chíreabháin from Conradh na Gaeilge for her advice.

I want to thank freelance press photographer Gareth Cheney for going to O'Connell Street to take photographs when I was locked down in Drogheda by Covid-19.

Thanks also to publisher Mary Feehan for her generosity regarding a photograph from the Mercier Press archive, and John Sheahan for allowing us to include the photograph of his grand-uncle, Patrick Sheahan.

And thanks to publisher Anthony Farrell for his generosity regarding a photograph from the Lilliput Press archive, and to author Peter Costello for sharing his sources and images from his research on Clerys and Denis Guiney.

Other folk who kindly helped me source photographs are Breeda Brennan from RTÉ Archives, Riccardo Cepach from Museo Sveviano in Trieste, James Harte from the National Library, Colum O'Riordan from the Irish Architectural Review, Lynn McDonnell from the Department of Local Housing, Government and Heritage Photo Archive, James Grange Osbourne from Independent News and Media and Glenn Dunne from the National Library.

As always, I am indebted to designer and artist Emma Byrne. She has designed most of my books, and her email containing her gorgeous cover was, once again, a marvellous boost on a day when I really needed to believe that the end was in sight and that there would be a finished book.

My editor of the last ten years Susan Houlden was her usual incredible self. This is our seventh book together and it has been a privilege to have her fulfil several roles as guide, teacher and supporter. I cannot thank her enough for all her help. This was a challenging book to put together and she was with me every step of the way.

Finally, credit must to go to my husband Niall Carney for listening to me talk about O'Connell Street for the last year or so.

Contents

O'Connell Street has proved itself as the prime location for momentous events in Ireland's history.

Author's Note

I have always believed that O'Connell Street tells the story of Ireland. Throughout its transformation from dirt path to the main thoroughfare of the capital city, O'Connell Street took centre stage, time and time again.

In 2016, retired architects Klaus Unger and Stephen Kane gave a lecture about O'Connell Street in Rathmines Library, in which they described its disentanglement from the warren that was medieval Dublin to establishing itself as the prime location for the momentous events of Ireland's twentieth-century history, beginning with the 1922 funeral of revolutionary and politician Michael Collins. Other events named were 1923's heavyweight boxing championship, that took place in La Scala Theatre, the 1932 Eucharistic Congress, the 1963 motorcade for President John Fitzgerald Kennedy's visit, not to mention several decades of St Patrick's Day parades.

However, plenty of historic moments had been played out before Michael Collin's funeral cortège slowly made its way down Sackville Street.

The architects pinpointed the street's first appearance on a map in 1728 when it was known as Drogheda Street. It was renamed Sackville Street in the 1740s by the new landowner Luke Gardiner who, over the next twenty years, oversaw the realisation of his vision that transformed the street into something very beautiful and beloved by seventeenth-century aristocracy and Victorian Anglo-Irish. They clamoured to buy up the newly built lavish houses, appreciating the area's architectural resemblance to London.

In 1814, Sackville Street saw the opening of a new General Post Office, in recognition of a growing population and economy. Just over one hundred years later, poet and headmaster Pádraig Pearse and his comrades chose this ornate building to make their stand for Irish freedom during the 1916 Easter Rising. How many soldiers lost their lives on this street?

Trade unionist James Larkin took to the balcony of the Imperial Hotel, unleashing hell one Sunday afternoon in 1913. Seven years after that, another dreadful Sunday in Irish history began with two shootings in the Gresham Hotel. Within a couple of years, the fires of battle returned, thanks to a civil war that, before it burnt out, wrapped itself around the hotels on O'Connell Street.

History is not buildings nor streets – at least, not by themselves. They only become important according to who they accommodate. So, history is people, and this street had a full cast: the very rich and the very poor – doctors, sculptors, architects, actors, writers, tailors, jewellers, booksellers, hoteliers, revolutionaries and lots and lots of traffic. In the 1990s, it even had its very own dancer in the always immaculate Mary Dunne who didn't care what anyone thought as she dipped and swayed to music only she could hear, the brightest smile on O'Connell Street. She told someone that she hated the Spire being built.

In his compelling *A Reluctant Memoir*, Irish artist Robert Ballagh (*b.* 1943) mentions an RTÉ interview with newspaper and business tycoon Gerry McGuinness (1939–2018) – whose working life began as house manager of the Carlton Cinema on O'Connell Street – in which McGuinness proposed that all the statues on O'Connell Street be torn down and replaced with modern Irish heroes, that is, his fellow business-men: Michael Smurfit, Ben Dunne and Tony O'Reilly. Ballagh disagreed with McGuinness's list but was propelled to consider who he felt should be celebrated, which is how his portrait of the former Minister for Health Noel Browne (1915–97) came about.

For my part, I can only hope that, by the time someone else writes another book about O'Connell Street, there will be statues commemorating Irish women.

Nicola Pierce

The restored chapter house of St Mary's Abbey.

CHAPTER ONE

A Brief Summary

ST MARY'S ABBEY

In perhaps its earliest guise, O'Connell Street was part of a vast estate belonging to St Mary's Abbey, Dublin's first Norse Christian foundation.

The Annals of Dublin record, for the year 1139, the founding of the Savigniac (Benedictine) Abbey of St Mary. The building was lauded as one of the finest in Dublin and its guesthouse the one favoured by important visitors to the city. Eight years later, it was taken over by Cistercian monks and, in 1156, was established as a daughter house (a dependant) of the Cistercian – formerly Savigniac – Buildwas Abbey in Shropshire, with the declaration (translated from Latin):

> We commit and submit to you and house the care and disposition of our house of St Mary, Dublin, to be held in perpetuity.

The abbey proved a lucrative business thanks to its approximately 30,000 acres that spread out from the river Liffey to the Tolka, incorporating Grangegorman, Glasnevin and parts of County Meath, after King Henry

II (1133–1189) visited Dublin in 1172 and gave St Mary's 'all the land of Clonlliffe as far as the Tolka'. Over a hundred houses, rented out to tenants, provided a steady income, while the abbey's own private quay and harbour allowed the monks to trade very successfully in salmon as well as produce from the acres of farmland. Furthermore, they ran a hostelry for medieval tourists. It also housed the biggest library in Ireland. Quite quickly, the abbey became the wealthiest religious house in Ireland.

Disaster hit temporarily in 1304 when a fire destroyed a number of buildings, including the church and belfry. However, the monks could afford to rebuild whatever was necessary, although many of the city's records were lost. Christine Casey, in her book *The Buildings of Ireland*, refers to the Abbey's cartularies (legal documents), from the fourteenth and fifteen centuries, as being full of details about the numerous and grand buildings. Government papers were stored in the Abbey in the fifteenth century and, because there were no government buildings in Ireland, it also provided the location for the meetings of the Irish Privy Council, senior advisors to the king or his representative.

A more serious disaster occurred in 1539, when King Henry VIII (1491–1547) dissolved the big monasteries, paying off the abbots and monks whilst confiscating all their properties and businesses. In hindsight, this was inevitable considering that the abbey was making over £500 a year, drawing the biggest income in Ireland and the third biggest between Britain and Ireland. Compare that to the annual £195 allotted to the treasurer of Dublin.

The library was quickly dispersed and mostly lost to Ireland. However, one manuscript, produced in the Abbey in the fourteenth century, went on sale in 2014. This was the first public sale of a medieval manuscript in a hundred years and Trinity College, determined to have it, put out a call for donations to aid them in their mission. They were overwhelmed by the generous response they received, including from strangers, which

Stephen Conlin artist's impression of St Mary's Abbey, c. 1450.

enabled them to place the winning bid at the Christie's auction and bring the manuscript 'home' to Ireland in 2015. It is made up of several writings, including those of the Norman archdeacon and historian Gerald of Wales's (1146–1223) *The History and Topography of Ireland*. He first visited Ireland in 1183 and clearly found himself much inspired, as when asked by an appreciative reader, Archbishop Baldwin of Canterbury (1125–1190), about his research methods, Gerald replied that he had merely relied on God's grace, which may explain various liberties taken regarding facts and figures.

Today all that remains of St Mary's Abbey is the twelfth-century chapter house (meeting room), a vaulted room beneath Meetinghouse Lane, off Capel Street. The room was rebuilt with strict adherence to its original detail thanks to the OPW (Office of Public Works). It is a hidden gem and is open to visitors.

In 1610, James I granted the land to Henry King, who held it for nine years. Following the Restoration of the Monarchy in 1660, when Charles II (1630–1685) returned from exile in Europe, the estate was passed on in perpetuity to the 1st Earl of Drogheda, Henry Moore (*d.* 1676). Henry, who was made Governor of Drogheda in 1660 and, the following year, was created Earl of Drogheda, moved into the Abbot's House and drew up plans to develop the area. Clearly wishing to be remembered, Henry had new streets laid out and named accordingly: Henry Street, Moore Street, Earl Street (now North Earl Street) and Drogheda Street. The land stayed in the Moore family for the next two generations until the death of the 3rd Earl of Drogheda, Henry's youngest son, also Henry (1660–1714), brought about the sale of the estate by Moore's trustees to Irish property developer Luke Gardiner (*c.* 1690–1755).

ALICE MOORE

Drogheda Street, the future O'Connell Street, made its first appearance on a map in 1728. Mostly residential, the street, which was typically narrow

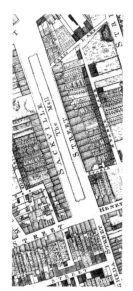

and short, was more of a lane and did not extend to the River Liffey. However, the street underwent a complete transformation in 1749 thanks to Luke Gardiner who ended up owning practically the entire area on the south side of the Liffey, as far as Fleet Street, following Sir Henry Moore's death in 1714. The names will be familiar, of course, but the story of Gardiner's acquisition begs to be told.

Rocque's map of 1756 shows the The Mall down the middle of the then Sackville Street and the many Georgian houses with long back gardens that filled Upper Sackville Street.

Like most things, it began with a woman. Alice Moore (*c.* 1622–1677) was Henry's sister, and in 1667 she married the 2nd Earl of Clanbrassil, Lord Henry Hamilton (1647–1675). Henry's hugely wealthy relatives were not in favour of the marriage, although Alice is described in their family records as 'very handsome, witty and well bred' just before she is declared immoral for entertaining all manner of men in her home, and bitterly criticised for her expensive tastes that almost bankrupted poor, besotted Henry. Three years later, in April 1670, a son was born, James, who lived barely two months before dying on 13 June.

Alice, it seems, was not content to be merely linked via marriage to Lord Henry's property because she convinced him to draw up a new will, making her the sole beneficiary. Henry's mother tried to caution him, warning that if he did what Alice wanted, he would end up prematurely lying beside his deceased father and brother. Henry should have listened to his mother. He died on 12 January 1675, leaving Alice fabulously rich and under suspicion of poisoning her husband in order to nab his estates. According to the family records, Henry died three months after changing his will and, furthermore, was disembowelled five hours after taking his last breath, just before a private burial in Christ Church. However, in an essay on seventeenth-century women in Louth, local historian Harold O'Sullivan points out that Henry's new will was dated 27 March 1674, ten months before he died in January 1675. The Hamilton family records are definitely far from objective; they really disliked Alice. In truth, we will never know if she was responsible for her husband's untimely death.

Her in-laws moved quickly to stymy her inheritance, claiming that an earlier will, written up by Henry's father, was the only valid document regarding the family property. Alice hung in, and a lengthy, expensive court case ensued, made especially more expensive when Alice sought to bribe anyone who might be of use to her. Her father, Henry, died almost a year to the day after her husband Henry, on 11 January 1676. That same year

Alice married again, this time to Scottish widower John Hamilton, 2nd Lord Bargeny (*c.* 1640–1693), but her new husband's brand of politics and hatred for King Charles II cost her a fortune. A payment of 50,000 merks (a Scottish silver coin) was made, either as a bribe or fine, to the king on 11 May 1680, to keep Bargeny out of jail. Furthermore, it cannot have been a good relationship since, following her own death in 1677, Alice left everything to her brother Henry, including the ongoing campaign for the Hamilton estate, which would result in seventeen more years of litigation. Henry proved as stubborn as his sister and, consequently, in 1681, spiralling legal costs obliged him to mortgage his estate to fellow developer Luke Gardiner. Finally, Alice's court case was concluded in the Hamiltons' favour. In other words, when her brother Henry died in 1714, Luke Gardiner inherited his property and a new age was born.

LUKE GARDINER

In *The Best Address in Town: Henrietta Street, Dublin and its First Residents, 1720–80* Melanie Hayes provides an engaging portrait of Luke Gardiner (*c.* 1690–1755). A self-made man, details about his early years are scant and, therefore, presumed humble. His father was either James Gardiner, from the Coombe, or merchant William Gardiner. Initially, it was believed that Luke began his working life as a footman for Mr White in Leixlip Castle. However, this has been disputed by historians who find this too fantastic considering his exceptional prowess with figures and paperwork. It is more reasonable to assume that he must have been a secretary or clerk of some kind.

Luke Gardiner, a man with a vision.

One of his earliest employers was John South, an English commissioner of the revenue in Ireland, who probably got him his first revenue post in 1708. From there, Gardiner worked his way up to secretary of the Dublin Ballast Office, before being promoted to hearths tax inspector (house owners were taxed on the number of fireplaces they had).

He married well, which suggests that he was accumulating wealth that

afforded him to move in aristocratic circles. This surely explains his marrying the fourteen-year-old niece of a viscount, the Honourable Anne
Stewart (1697–1753) in 1711. The following year, he opened up his own
bank with the Right Honourable Arthur Hill (*c.* 1694–1771), which had a
successful run until 1738 when Gardiner decided to concentrate on politics.

By this stage, he had a stream of positions and titles to his name, including his 1722 appointment as trustee of the Royal Barracks (now Collins
Barracks). As a patron of Dublin's art and culture scene, he joined all
kinds of boards and public bodies, which served to expand his social
standing in the community and resulted in his inviting lord lieutenants
to dine with him.

Success followed him wherever he went. His entrance into politics in
1723, becoming MP for Tralee and then Thomastown, culminated in his
taking a seat on the Privy Council in 1737.

His first excursion into real estate involved buying up land around the
South Lotts, in 1712. The North and South Lotts were reclaimed marsh-
lands that had been created with the embankment of the River Liffey in
1711. What followed over the next forty years was a string of property
deals that saw him acquiring tracts of land either side of the Liffey. The
enormous acquisition of the Moore estate put him into debt, and Melanie
Hayes surmises that this was why he did not develop the land for another
twenty years.

Hayes portrays him as an indulgent parent to his four surviving children,
two sons and two daughters. Neither son showed much interest in business,
though they enjoyed the life of luxury provided by their father. However,
Luke's grandson, and namesake, Luke (1745–1798), would continue on
with his grandfather's work.

A man of vision and creativity, Gardiner set out between 1748 and 1750
to develop Upper Drogheda Street, which was, at that time, a narrow, dingy
street. He tore down the houses on its west side in order to widen the street

to over 150 feet (45.7 metres), making it twice the width of neighbouring streets. Next, he built approximately 400 houses, big and small, around the upper end of Sackville Street, from Henry Street to Parnell Square, and would have liked to extend this development as far as the Liffey but he did not own any property south of Sackville Street. At this time, the street was closed at the south end with no direct way through to College Green. In 1750, he built a 890-yard (814-metre) long, 492-foot (150-metre) wide mall, enclosed by a 4-foot (1.21-metre) wall, down its centre. This enclosed promenade was for ladies and gentlemen who wished to take exercise in safety from the potential dangers of carriage wheels or runaway horses. Initially, the game of mall would have been played here, whereby players, equipped with a heavy wooden mallet, hit a small ball through an iron hoop. The winner achieved this with the fewest hits. When the game fell out of fashion, trees were planted to fill out the space. The tree-lined mall was decorated with obelisks, globes and lamps that must have made it a pretty sight on a winter's evening.

Gardiner had created a prestigious private estate.

SACKVILLE STREET AND THE WIDE STREETS COMMISSION

Signalling a new era, Gardiner changed the name Drogheda Street to Sackville Street in the late 1740s in tribute to English aristocrat Lionel Sackville (1688–1765), two-times lord lieutenant of Ireland and the 1st Duke of Dorset. He also named one of his sons Sackville (*d.* 1796), which suggests that the families were close. Meanwhile, the new houses that he built were being eagerly claimed by the best sort of people, the upper class, professional men and members of parliament; for example, the architect and Deputy Ranger of the Phoenix Park, Nathaniel Clements (1707–1777), who built a Ranger's Lodge for himself in the park, which has since become Áras an Uachtaráin, the official residence of the President of Ireland.

Lionel Sackville (1688–1765), two-times Lord Lieutenant of Ireland.

Other prominent Sackville neighbours included Alderman Richard Dawson, a prosperous banker, revenue commissioner and MP for Kilkenny, who lived in a splendid mansion that encompassed numbers nine and ten, with highly decorative rococo interiors and statues of eagles on its roof. When he died in 1766, his son sold his house for £5,000 to Charles Moore, 6th Earl of Drogheda (1730–1822), who racked up fierce gambling debts as a member of the elitist Hellfire Club, a social club for rich, pleasure-seeking young men. His new house became known as Drogheda House, and Charles may have appreciated the stone eagles on the parapet as a discreet nod to his social life, considering that the Eagle Tavern in Cork Street was the favourite meeting place for the Hell Fire crowd.

Charles's famous ancestor, Henry Moore, the 1st Earl of Drogheda and 3rd Viscount Moore, had previously built himself a mansion between Earl Street and today's Cathedral Street.

Another neighbour was MP of Randalstown John Dunn, whose private art collection included *The Holy Family* by Peter Paul Rubens (1577–1640).

In 1750, MP for Louth Henry Bellingham (*c.* 1713–1755) and his wife Margaret Henry moved into number 18 Sackville Street, which was designed by Richard Cassels. Mrs Bellingham outlived her husband and died in April 1764, after which the house became the town residence for Peter Browne, 2nd Earl of Altamont (*c.* 1731–1780), an Irish landowner and MP. He was clearly a wealthy man since he kept fifteen servants in his Sackville Street house, which was five more than most other houses. This is where the English writer Thomas de Quincey (1785–1859) stayed on his visit to Dublin, just before the rebellion in 1798 and his breakout success in 1821 with his addiction memoir, *Confessions of an English Opium-Eater*.

One of the houses destined to become part of the original Gresham Hotel was home to Sir Thomas Yeates, who assisted the master and surgeon Dr Bartholomew Mosse in the Rotunda. Its interior was reputed to be the most beautiful in the city and one of the most social, hosting the best parties.

Lady Catherine Netterville (1712–1784) moved into Sackville Street in 1771. Four years later, eight or nine armed men broke in and abducted her granddaughter Catherine Blake. A reward was offered for her safe return and the story ended well as young Catherine went on to marry Anthony Atkinson (*d.* 1815). Furthermore, on 27 March 1771, a warrant was issued for the arrest of a James Mulcail Moore, alias James Mulhall, and companions, for 'forcibly carrying away' Catherine from her grandmother's home.

The abduction appears in the 1907 book *The Story of Dublin*, by historian David Alfred Chart, who uses it to highlight the inefficiency of the city's community watch.

The July 1957 edition of the *Dublin Historical Record* series includes an essay by Mrs JF Daly, entitled 'O'Connell Bridge and Its Environs'. She references the eighteenth-century journal, the *Dublin Chronicle*, of May 1787, which tells of an enormous statue of Neptune (the Roman God of the Sea) that was presented to Sackville, the Lord Lieutenant of Ireland. Plans were submitted for the construction of a fountain in Sackville Street and the statue was to be a feature. Furthermore, in October 1787, a meeting was held to discuss the possibility of having a statue of the River God created for Sackville Street. It was not to be as the council could not reach an agreement on its design or location.

However, the fountain was built where the Parnell Monument stands today. In 1789, a guide to Dublin was published in which the author, Lewis, describes the fountain as 'elegant' and 'remarkable'. It lasted until 1807 when the Pavement Commission had it removed following several accidents during the winter months when the residual water iced over, making the area hazardous for pedestrians and horses alike.

In their lecture about O'Connell Street, architects Klaus Unger and Stephen Kane used the word 'amenity' to summarise Gardiner's Sackville creation, referring to the street's unique look thanks to the houses differing in size and appearance. They quote Irish architectural historian Maurice

Craig (1919–2011), who described Gardiner's mall as an 'elongated square' because the residents would have enjoyed complete privacy from the rest of the city and its inhabitants.

The houses were like showpieces for their owners as their exteriors conveyed grandeur, hinting at the riches within. One house which has survived from this time, number 42 Upper O'Connell Street, allows the architects to point out the use of Portland stone and decorative touches around the front door that provide an immediate 'impression of elegance'. The need for another bridge became obvious once those grand houses filled up in Upper Sackville Street. Several of the new residents were parliamentarians and were obliged to make a long detour to cross over the Liffey at Essex Bridge in order to reach Parliament House in College Green.

Later on, the Wide Streets Commissioners, established in 1757, added their own improvements, opening up the south end of Sackville Street and extending it to meet the new Carlisle Bridge (now O'Connell Bridge) that replaced a ferry in the 1790s.

Indeed, the travel writer John Bush, whose book *Hibernia Curiosa* was based on his tour of Ireland in 1764, and included his complaints about heavy drinking and shambolic public transport, believed that had Sackville Street stretched all the way to the river, it would easily be one of the most beautiful streets in Europe. In any case, it was the first boulevard built in Ireland and the British Isles.

The names of the gentlemen commissioners will be familiar to those with an interest in Dublin's history: Arran, Burgh, Clanbrassil, Kildare, Leinster and so on, all bound together by an interest in architecture, wealth and a desire to beautify the capital city according to *their* tastes which were largely inspired by Paris and London. In fact, they had a map of London on the wall of their meeting room. Nothing impeded their vision. For instance, the first street they worked on, now Parliament Street, was home to some folk who had changed their mind about selling up and moving out.

Most were in bed when the commissioners' demolition team arrived. First thing the residents knew about it was when the roofs were torn from their houses, sending them running outside, in the belief that the city was under attack – which in a way it was, albeit in the name of progress.

The commissioners had the law on their side, with several acts of parliament extending their powers to do as they saw fit, including a 1790 Act that actually regulated the proper style in which a house was to be built; that is, it was to blend in with the neighbours. Thanks to them, Sackville Street was rejuvenated, not least because of its new status as an integral part of the rite of passage from the Rotunda Hospital all the way to St Stephen's Green. Three of the commissioners were also governors of the hospital, resulting in its own transformation that included a new entrance specifically designed to be seen from Sackville Street.

Gary A Boyd in his book *Dublin, 1745–1922* writes that some saw the commissioners' redevelopment of Sackville Street as proof of an underlying desire to create an elite and separate Protestant city within the city of Dublin. The architecture, the newly arranged streets of like-minded neighbours that were now linked without obstacle, along with the likes of Gardiner's Mall, reflected the wealth and culture of its dominant resident, the affluent and influential Protestant. Is it coincidental that during this time the word 'Ascendancy' was now applied to the Anglo-Irish ruling class? Irish merchant and Catholic radical John Keogh (1740–1817) quipped that one could recognise a Catholic Dubliner from how he 'slunk' up a street that probably felt alien to him. In any case, the commissioners did what they set out to do. When the artist James Malton visited Dublin in the late 1790s, he declared Sackville Street to be 'the noblest street in Europe, inhabited by persons of the first rank and opulence'.

Following the Act of Union in 1800 and the termination of the Irish Parliament, Ireland would now be ruled from Westminster, a number of aristocratic residents sold up and moved back to London.

Sackville Street, c. 1750s, by James Malton.

Twelve years later, nineteen-year-old poet Percy Bysshe Shelley (1792–1822), an English aristocrat, his sixteen-year-old wife, Harriet (1796–1816) and her twenty-nine-year-old sister, Eliza, arrived in Sackville Street on 12 February, determined to rouse the natives into throwing off their colonial shackles. The Shelleys abhorred their country's harsh record regarding Ireland. Making their home on the first floor of 7 Sackville Street (now the Bank of Ireland), Shelley went in search of a printer for his pamphlet, 'An address to the Irish People'. Impatient to be of service to the working class, he flung copies of his address from the window of his lodgings as well as posting it to all important persons and having bundles of it delivered to local pubs and coffee houses.

Percy Bysshe Shelley lived on Sackville Street for two months in 1812.

In her essay, 'The Shelleys in Ireland', biographer Eleanor Fitzsimons provides several reasons for Shelley's devotion to Ireland, including the fact that he had been a neighbour of Lord Edward Fitzgerald's (1763–98) half-sister in Sussex. Irish parliamentarian, and United Irishman, Fitzgerald had helped organise the 1798 rebellion but was fatally wounded mid-arrest the night before it was to take place. The only Irish person to take Shelley seriously was Catherine Nugent (*b.* 1771–1847), a seamstress who had taken part in the rebellion. An ardent and committed nationalist, Nugent had read Shelley's pamphlet and arrived at number 7 Sackville Street to acquaint herself with its author. She and Harriet would become firm friends, while she encouraged Percy to branch out from his fixation with the lower classes and endeavour to win the minds of Dublin's intellectuals.

In any case, he accomplished little, being out of step with those who mattered. His pamphlet was too long and found patronising in tone, whilst his warnings to steer clear of the demon drink were not appreciated. The poet and his family returned to England two months later, frustrated by their inability to affect any kind of change but proud that they had at least tried.

When poet Oliver St John Gogarty's Galway home, Renvyle House, was burnt to the ground during Ireland's Civil War, he reflected upon its loss in his memoir, *As I Was Going Down Sackville Street*, remembering the variety of guests he hosted, from the Welsh artist Augustus John (1878–1961) to William Butler Yeats (1865–1939) and that the house was haunted. One night, Evan Morgan, a Welsh psychic, along with six others saw the ghost of Percy Shelley 'with his long, white open neck, high forehead, chestnut hair and aquamarine eyes'.

There is, it seems, always unfinished business for those who love Ireland.

In 1813, the popular Anglo-Irish writer Maria Edgeworth (1768–1849) records her guests' comments about Dublin. Wealthy industrialist and philanthropist Joseph Strutt (1765–1844), from Derbyshire, thought Dublin to be far prettier than London.

Two years later, in 1815, another visitor to Sackville Street, William Gregory, complimented the street for its resemblance to London, writing that 'a stranger from that city might imagine he was in London'.

The grandeur of the GPO and Nelson's Pillar is emphasised by the unpaved street in this early photograph.

Gary A Boyd suggests that the construction of the GPO and Nelson's Pillar, which happened after the 1800 Act of Union, was a discreet act of imperialism. Yes, they were very beautiful but, in reality, the post office was built to house British administration, while Nelson had no connections to Ireland. Early nineteenth-century Sackville Street, he feels, even as it bloomed with these marvellous additions, was celebrating Dublin losing its status as an Irish capital city and, therefore, becoming something less than that.

An intriguing description of Luke Gardiner's Mall appeared in a society paper in August 1809:

> Here the rich and the poor and the giddy of each sex resort – here they take the dust by way of taking the air, straining their eyes to gaze at Nelson.

That mention of the 'poor' is a reminder of those others who lived within walking distance of MPs and bankers. Dublin was a busy city after all. In his article about prostitution on 1870s Grafton Street, historian Donal Fallon quotes from a letter written to the *Freeman's Journal* at the time, in which the author suggests a solution that worked well the previous summer on Sackville Street, whereby six men from G-Division (Dublin's intelligence police) should patrol Grafton Street between four and six o'clock every day.

By 1850, Sackville Street was undergoing another transformation as more businesses moved in and erected gaudy shopfronts to advertise their wares, thus dismantling Gardiner's, and the Wide Streets Commissioners', original vision of a united front of grand houses. One consequence of this was that the street felt more inclusive and so the beggars now frequented the street, while prostitutes solicited their wares beneath the portico of the GPO.

In the late 1800s an earnest attempt was undertaken to 'make' Dublin more Irish. Dublin Corporation turned its attention to Sackville Street, voting in 1884 to rename it in honour of Daniel O'Connell. However, irate residents put a stop to this plan with a court injunction. Twenty-seven years later, the corporation succeeded in renaming Rutland Square and Great Britain Street after Charles Stewart Parnell. More of the same would only occur following independence in 1921 and, incredibly, three more years would pass before Sackville Street became O'Connell Street.

LONG-RUNNING RETAIL HISTORY

In his 2001 essay about Sackville Street, geographer Doctor Joseph Brady is critical of the street both then and now, claiming that it lost something when it was widened and joined up with the south part of the city. He offers the year 1911 as a highlight in the street's history, thanks to the likes of Clery's Department Store and Eason's, alongside a variety of businesses on Lower Sackville Street such as chemists, opticians and The Happy Ring House jewellers. Many of these shops had an upmarket sibling branch on Grafton Street in recognition that there were two types of customers, northside and southside. Hotels included the Metropole, the Waverley, the Grand and the Imperial Hotel, which shared a building with Clery's.

Upper Sackville Street might have appeared sedate in comparison, with fewer retail outlets aside from Tyler's shoe shop at number 1, which makes its first appearance in *Thom's Official Directory* in 1902, and Lawrence photographic studio at numbers 5–7, which opened opposite the GPO in March 1865. More than a few doors away, at numbers 28–32, was Findlater's headquarters, their large anchor shop, to which was added, in 1927, a delicatessen and a confectionary. Established in 1774, they sold imported teas, wine, beers and spirits that were stored in large cellars beneath Sackville Street. It is interesting to note that John Head, who worked there for thirty years before becoming a senior partner, chose to live on the southside of the

Above: Findlater's headquarters at 28–32 Sackville Street.
Below: The Christmas rush, Findlater's, in the 1960s.

city, renting different houses in the Leeson Street area. The consummate shopper was obliged to go to Henry Street because Upper Sackville Street had little to offer apart from financial institutions such as the Northern and Royal Bank and insurance companies. Other inhabitants were social clubs like the Sackville Street Club and a range of religious societies including the Presbyterian Association, the Catholic Truth Society and the Hibernian Bible Society. Hotels-wise, the Gresham and the Hamman were the best known but only the Gresham would survive the Civil War. Until then, however, the Hamman Hotel boasted about their in-house Turkish Baths.

Other businesses included A&R Thwaites & Company, who claimed to have invented soda water. Set up in 1799, at number 57, this company may also have instigated the first example of recycling when they advertised paying two shillings for every dozen returned bottles.

O'CONNELL STREET TODAY

Over two hundred years later, the street is looking tired and neglected. In 2019 plans were submitted to redevelop Upper O'Connell Street and its empty, some derelict, buildings. Ironically, it is a UK property company, Hammerson, who were given approval to transform waste ground beside the Carlton unit. Their plans for the upper part of O'Connell Street also stretch back to Moore Street. They are working with three Irish architect firms, Grafton, MOLA and RKD, and plans include restoring number 42, the last Georgian building to survive on the street. Built in the 1750s, its original owner was former State Physician Robert Robinson (1713–70), who, as Professor of Anatomy in Trinity College, had his students discreetly crash a wake in order to rob the corpse for class. The deceased was the Tipperary giant Cornelius Magrath (1736–60), and Robinson had chosen him as he longed to dissect a figure with such a massive frame.

Number 42 Upper O'Connell Street, the last remaining Georgian house, now a protected building.

CHALLENGES FOR THE FUTURE

Mindful of the surrounding area's role in 1916, Hammerson also plan to create a historical trail about The Rising, as part of their effort to change yet preserve the historical context of O'Connell and Moore Streets.

The closing of Clery's was a crucial loss to the street but, Covid-19 restrictions aside, construction has begun that will see the building converted into a state-of-the-art multiplex with office and retail space, a hotel and a restaurant. So, while retaining its iconic façade, Clery's will reopen but in a new way, just like the trams returned to O'Connell Street in 2017, albeit via their thoroughly modern descendant the Luas.

These developments will return long absent people to the area – shoppers, tourists and office workers. Some may worry that O'Connell Street will lose its authenticity, that the modern facelifts aspire to compare favourably with major streets in other capital cities and, perhaps, this is inevitable. But change is needed and surely it is an acknowledgement of the street's importance that these plans were ever sought?

The Daniel O'Connell Monument, which was unveiled on a wet Tuesday in August 1882, has a birds-eye view of O'Connell Street.

CHAPTER TWO

Statues and Monuments

DANIEL O'CONNELL

Today, many believe that Daniel O'Connell (1775–1847) was Ireland's greatest politician. The O'Connell Monument sits across from O'Connell Bridge and is possibly the first thing that a visitor notices on their approach to the lower end of O'Connell Street.

O'Connell's momentous achievements include his reawakening the poor tenant farmers and the Catholic middle class who had fallen into a stupor, succumbing to the restrictions imposed on their congregation by the British Empire, whereby Catholics were barred from the British parliament and, therefore, none ever stood for election.

In 1823, O'Connell set up the Catholic Association with its 'Catholic Rent' of a penny a month that allowed the poorest Catholic to join its ranks and, in this way, he may have created the world's first mass democratic union. In 1828, he decided to make his move, presenting himself on the ballot ticket in a by-election in County Clare. He was curious to see what would happen if he won. It seemed that the population of Ireland collectively recognised the potential of this moment, obeying an unofficial order not to cause any trouble that might affect the outcome. Pubs closed, nobody drank or picked a fight and O'Connell was elected by a large majority, forcing the hand of the British government, who were obliged to push through the Emancipation Act of 1829. This triumph resulted in O'Connell being called 'The Emancipator' or 'The Great Liberator', although King George's (1762–1830) response went a little further than that. After the act was passed, the king remarked sourly that Daniel O'Connell was now the real king of Ireland.

In later years, Daniel O'Connell joked that the fact his birth coincided with the American War of Independence (1775–1783) was surely a sign that he would become a champion of freedom.

His wealthy uncle sent him off to France to finish his education in 1790, inadvertently landing him in the middle of revolution. What the young Daniel saw and experienced during the French Revolution (1789–1799) ensured that he would always advocate political gain by peaceful means only.

Perhaps his greatest moment took place on 15 August 1834 when up to a million Irishmen, women and children attended a mass meeting on the Hill of Tara to hear him speak. He was undoubtedly aware that he was standing on hallowed ground, where Ruaidrí Ua Conchobair (Roderick O'Connor) (1116–1198) had been crowned High King of Ireland in 1170.

Even his critics fell under his spell. William Howard Russell (1820–1907), one of Ireland's (and the world's) first war correspondents, who opposed O'Connell's repeal stance, wrote in his journal:

I have never heard any orator who made so great an impression on me as O'Connell. It was not his argument, for it was often worthless, nor his language, which was frequently inelegant. It was his immense passion, his path, his fiery indignation.

Times journalist William Howard Russell was a reluctant fan of Daniel O'Connell.

O'Connell's legendary brilliance in oration and agitation extended beyond Irish shores. Indeed, four years earlier when Belgian parliamentarians were voting for a new king, three of them voted for Daniel O'Connell. Then, when black abolitionist Frederick Douglass (1818–95) visited Ireland in 1845, he was already a fan thanks to O'Connell's vehement condemnation of slavery; O'Connell had criticised George Washington for owning slaves and had declared that he would never visit America until slavery was abolished.

Frederick Douglass became firm friends with Daniel O'Connell during his visit to Ireland in 1845.

In 1840, O'Connell attended the first World Anti-Slavery Convention in London and there he encountered another group in need of defending. The organisers were ignoring a group of American women who had arrived to take part in the convention and had found themselves marginalised by their gender. Typically, O'Connell opposed their treatment, arguing for equality in the battle against slavery, declaring that 'Mind has no sex'.

The following year he struck a peaceful blow for Irish Catholics when he became the first Catholic Lord Mayor of Dublin in a hundred and fifty years.

Following a short term of imprisonment at Richmond Bridewell Penitentiary in 1844, after being convicted for 'conspiracy', O'Connell's blistering reign of popularity crumbled. His influence was waning due to a combination of old age and ill health that was possibly caused by heartbreak over the famine and his being overtaken by the Young Irelanders, who favoured violence in opposing British rule in Ireland.

He made his last speech in the British House of Commons on 8 February 1847, begging for relief for his people, whose numbers were being devastated by famine and mass emigration. He championed Conservative politician Lord George Bentinck's (1802–1848) bill to empower the government into lending sixteen million pounds to the Irish railway companies, thereby providing employment and wages for a starving population as well as opening Ireland up for further development.

In obvious failing health, he could not make himself heard as he predicted that a quarter of the population of Ireland would die if the British government did not step up and provide the money. With his old zeal extinguished, O'Connell's pleas went largely unnoticed. It was a far cry from the orator whose style, as a 'pleader', was described by an English admirer as:

> The best perhaps ever known ... Others have been more polished, more elegant ... but for clear force, for adroit invention, for the Demosthenic terseness, concentrating and controlling Irish fervour, for the impetuous hailstorm of words beating down resistance, we doubt whether any speaker of a nation has been the master of O'Connell.

The bill's failure to pass was a severe blow and, two days later, it was rumoured that Daniel O'Connell had died. In fact, the rumours were not so greatly exaggerated as O'Connell's health, both physical and mental, was breaking down. His political life was over. He thought to return to Ireland but decided that he needed a warmer climate and so, on 21 March, he sailed to Boulogne, on his way to Rome to be blessed by Pope Pius IX (1792–1878).

In Paris, he was diagnosed with an ever-worsening congestion of the brain. He felt constantly cold, while his utter feebleness convinced him that death was near. Crowds followed him wherever he went and local dignitaries sent their calling cards but he was unable to accept any invitations. When someone expressed a wish that he would recover, O'Connell told him that he might die within the next three days.

Then, for a couple of days, it seemed that he was improving. Arriving in Genoa on 6 May, he appeared well until a fierce headache beset him on the ninth which he blamed on an injection administered to him by a Doctor Lacour. After that, he refused all medicine. His last days were scrappily documented by John Duggan, his faithful manservant, and make for unpleasant reading. Leeches were applied to the back of his ears, there were enemas, blisters and poultices applied to various limbs; there are also notes on his inability to eat and his falling in and out of consciousness.

He had a terrible fear of being buried alive, and on Thursday, 13 May, he begged Duggan to make absolutely sure that he was dead before he was taken away for burial. Finally, Daniel O'Connell was released from his agonies at 9.30pm, Saturday 15 May.

In her *The Liberator: His Life and Times*, Sister Mary Francis Cusack (1829–1899) describes how O'Connell's funeral in Rome required the employing of 'artisans, sculptors, painters and architects' for a most lavish production that involved a four-hour sermon by orator priest Gioacchino Ventura di Raulica (1792–1861).

With his heart literally left behind in Rome, O'Connell's remains reached Ireland in August, where preparations were underway for his second funeral. On 5 August, thousands of grieving spectators turned out to watch Daniel O'Connell make his final journey from the Metropolitan Church in Marlborough Street up Westmoreland and Sackville Streets on his way to the cemetery he had helped establish in Glasnevin. It was the biggest funeral in Ireland's history at that time.

His statue was commissioned in 1862 by Dublin Corporation, with the granite foundation finally laid two years later amidst an unsuccessful search for an appropriate artist. Finally, in 1866, Dublin-born John Henry Foley (1818–1874) was asked to create the monument in celebration of 'The Liberator'.

Foley had a flair for capturing his subject in a characteristic pose. For example, his 1866 statue of dramatist and novelist Oliver Goldsmith, which is located outside the College Green entrance to Trinity College Dublin, stands with head bowed as if thoroughly absorbed in his book. Nearby can be found Foley's 1868 statue of Anglo-Irish statesman and campaigner Edmund Burke, striking a defiant stance, while the sculptor's 1876 statue of Henry Grattan shows the orator mid-speech.

Foley had left Ireland in 1835 to attend the Royal Academy in London and was judged to be the most talented sculptor of his day. One of his most important works was his gold statue of Prince Albert (1819–1861). Foley's depiction of her husband was a hit with Queen Victoria (1819–1901), with several of his pieces ending up in the Royal Collections. What would O'Connell have made of that? Actually, he might have been fine considering that he had helped organise the visit of King George IV (1762–1830), the queen's predecessor, to Ireland in 1821, even kneeling to present a laurel to him.

While Foley's talent could not be questioned, more than a few lamented over the O'Connell commission been given to a 'London artist' whose Irishness 'begins and ends with his name'. Sensitive to the criticism, those who commissioned the monument tried to limit Foley to the O'Connell figure alone. He began making notes and sketches for the work that he would not live to finish. In a way, the committee got their wish as Foley only completed the figure and the frieze. It was his assistant Thomas Brock (1847–1922) who sculpted the four-winged Victories after Foley's death.

The monument was unveiled on a rainy Tuesday, 15 August 1882, thirty-five years after its subject's death and is a marvel in itself. Four massive winged figures represent O'Connell's patriotism, courage, eloquence and fidelity. Above them is a circular frieze of thirty figures in high relief, each depicting an aspect of Irish life, including the 'Maid of Erin' who, stands on chains, holding the 1829 Act of Catholic Emancipation in one hand and, with the other, points heavenwards, directing us to look higher again. And there he stands, tall and proud: the former Lord Mayor of Dublin, lauded for peacefully liberating the Irish Catholic, although he lost the ultimate prize of repealing the Act of Union.

In his essay for the *Dublin Historical Record* series, Dr John Turpin (*b.* 1945) describes the monument as a 'masterpiece of complicated orchestration', pointing out how the 'voluminous cloak' ensures that the figure stands out and that 'a moving rhythm' is created by the drapery in the frieze.

The stack of books at the figure's feet along with the scroll in his right hand reference O'Connell's love of learning and his preference for words over bullets. He devoted his life to his fellow countrymen, women and children, wanting to free them from English rule while also urging America to free its slaves. Furthermore, he believed that a woman's contribution to a cause like the anti-slavery movement was as valuable as his own.

In 2005, when Dublin City Council had the monument cleaned, a team spent a thousand hours scrubbing away over a century's worth of smoke, graffiti and bird droppings. Of the thirty bullet holes found, ten decorated the statue itself with two through his right temple, thus reminding us that it literally bore witness to Easter 1916, the War of Independence and the Civil War.

The monument stood on Sackville Street for forty-two years until Dublin Corporation proposed a name change, seeing an opportunity to do so before new street signs were erected. The idea was to pay homage to big historical events and famous Irish names. Panic

One of the figures, Fidelity and her faithful hound, at the base of the Daniel O'Connell statue.

The only known photograph of
Daniel O'Connell, taken in 1844.

broke out amongst the street's residents who were convinced that a name change would herald disaster for their various occupations and businesses. However, the re-naming went ahead thanks to the Dublin Corporation Act of 1890 and on 5 May 1924, Sackville Street became O'Connell Street.

In October 2019, the National Gallery launched its exhibition, 'View of Ireland: Collecting Photography', which included the only known daguerreotype, or photograph, of Daniel O'Connell. The image was one hundred and seventy-five years old and taken by commercial photographer Chevalier Doussin Dubreuil (*fl.* 1842–1845), whose studio, in 1842, was on the roof of the Rotunda in Upper Sackville Street. In 1844, he was permitted inside the Bridewell Penitentiary (now Griffith College) to take the likeness of repeal prisoners such as O'Connell and Charles Gavan Duffy. O'Connell is wearing his green velvet 'Repeal' cap which is adorned with golden shamrocks. The image, which is small, is blurred thanks to someone making an ill-advised attempt to clean it.

Photography had been invented just five years earlier by Louis-Jacques-Mandé Daguerre (1787–1851), in France, and early sitters were required to sit still for ten minutes to allow the plate to be suitably exposed. In fact, Dubreuil's studio previously belonged to Richard Beard (1801–1885), who is probably responsible for bringing this new technology to Ireland

and his native Britain. Photography became a prosperous business and, less than twenty years later, the 1862 street directories listed three separate photographers for Lower Sackville Street and one at the other end of the street.

WILLIAM SMITH O'BRIEN

Thomas Farrell's (1827–1900) memorial to William Smith O'Brien (1803–1864), the Young Irelander, was unveiled at the O'Connell Bridge entrance to D'Olier Street on 26 December 1870, where it stood for almost sixty years before being moved to O'Connell Street in 1929. Standing tall on a granite pedestal, O'Brien is depicted wearing a frock-coat with his arms crossed, holding a scroll. *The Times* newspaper queried the point of the monument in 1870: 'Why gibbet such a failure in monumental marble?' Whatever your opinion about the 'failure' that was the 1798 rebellion, this was the first time in Dublin that someone who had physically opposed British rule was celebrated.

Educated at Harrow School and Cambridge's Trinity College, William Smith O'Brien had an English accent, was upper class, a Protestant and a landlord, no less. However, he was also a descendant of Brian Boru. Initially, supporting both Catholic Emancipation and the British-Ireland union, he converted to Daniel O'Connell's repeal movement in 1843 until the horror of the Famine made him and his Young Irelander friends unwilling to remain peaceful and patient in opposing British rule.

Young Irelander William Smith O'Brien.

The year 1848 was a pivotal one and the Young Irelanders felt inspired as governments throughout Europe were toppled by revolutions. If it worked for France, Germany, Italy and the Austrian Empire, to mention a few, it should surely work here in Ireland. O'Brien was much influenced by Londonderry-born John Mitchel (1815–1875).

The son of a Presbyterian minister, Mitchel founded *The United Irishmen* newspaper and yearned for, and loudly predicted, an Irish revolution – a 'holy war' to rid Ireland of all things British. When his fighting words led to his arrest and exile to Van Diemen's Land (Tasmania), it was William Smith O'Brien who stepped forward to make Mitchel's prophecy a reality.

Historian Robert Kee writes about O'Brien's inadequacies as a militant leader, surmising he was too much of the country gentleman. Nevertheless, in the summer of 1848, O'Brien found himself in Tipperary drumming up support for a rebellion. In fact, he raised quite an army – approximately 6,000 men from Wexford, Kilkenny and Tipperary – but while he could give them reason and passion to fight, he could not feed nor arm them. Although, perhaps he could have, had he agreed to seize provisions and private property as urged to by his colleagues, but his morality got in the way. Consequently, his men's weapons were pitchforks and pikes and they were hungry. He sent them home, telling them to fetch enough food for four days, an impossibility for most of them who failed to return.

On 27 July, O'Brien's now meagre forces were supplemented by Terence Bellow McManus's (1823–60) band of volunteers, who hailed from Liverpool. From County Fermanagh, McManus, a successful shipping agent in Liverpool, joined the Young Irelanders in 1844. In the village of Ballingarry, in 1848, he and his men, along with O'Brien, prepared to confront armed police who had been tasked with arresting O'Brien for treason.

The constables, suspecting themselves outnumbered, took shelter in a two-storey cottage with a cabbage patch and set about barricading the windows. O'Brien and his men gathered outside but before they could do anything, a woman arrived on the scene. On hearing how her house was occupied and being torn apart, Widow (Margaret) McCormack set up a cry about her five children who were in bed. O'Brien called a truce and approached a window of the house to discuss the safe exit of Mrs McCormack's youngsters. He took the opportunity to explain that, as an Irishman and a soldier, he only wanted the police officers' weapons. He promised to protect their lives and granted them five minutes to surrender but the officers refused to hand over either children or weapons. A stand-off might have ensued except that a couple of rebels began throwing stones at the house in frustration. Nervous officers retaliated with two volleys of fire, killing at least one rebel and severely injuring another. News of another police force on its way to lend assistance to those holed up in Widow McCormack's house panicked O'Brien's forces and they made their escape. The rebellion was over before it had begun and, in some quarters, would always be known as 'The Battle of Widow McCormack's Cabbage Patch'. Yet, a stand had finally been made, thus raising the bar for opposing British rule.

Widow McCormack's House, the scene of a brief battle in 1848.

Ultimately, O'Brien had risked his life for his country. Upon his arrest at Thurles train station and subsequent trial in Clonmel, he was sentenced as follows:

> To be hanged by the neck until he be dead and that afterwards his head should be severed from his body and his body divided into four quarters to be disposed of as Her Majesty should think fit.

However, public outcry saved O'Brien and, on 5 June 1849, his sentence was commuted to exile to Van Diemen's Land, where he flourished for the next five years thanks to the funds sent over from his estate in Cahirmoyle.

SIR JOHN GRAY

Originally from Claremorris in County Clare, Sir John Gray (1815–75) started out as a physician in 1839, taking a position in a hospital on North Cumberland Street, Dublin. Before long, he found himself writing for newspapers and becoming involved with nationalist politics, throwing his

Physician, journalist and politician Sir John Gray.

full support behind Daniel O'Connell and, later on, Charles Stewart Parnell.

His statue stands on O'Connell Street upper, just behind his hero Daniel O'Connell.

Sculptor Thomas Farrell also created this monument which was unveiled on 24 June 1879 by Tuam's Catholic Archbishop John MacHale (1789–1881). The location on Sackville Street was chosen for its proximity to the Abbey Street offices of Gray's newspaper the *Freeman's Journal*. MacHale and Gray had much in common; both supported Daniel O'Connell's repeal movement and set out to right society's wrongs as they saw them. The Catholic archbishop demanded that his clergy spoke Irish and worked tirelessly for Catholic emancipation. He also demanded justice for the poor and the downtrodden tenants, and vehemently opposed the government's proposal for non-sectarian primary schools. In time, he would have his own statue sculpted by Thomas Farrell, which stands at Tuam Cathedral, County Galway.

A fictional account of the unveiling of the Gray statue turns up in James Joyce's short story 'Grace', from the *Dubliners* collection and is far from complimentary about the Gray family and Archbishop McHale. 'None of the Grays was any good' declares one of Joyce's characters, while another describes the Archbishop as a 'crabbed-looking old chap' with bushy eyebrows.

Gray, a Protestant and a nationalist, had been on the committee that called for the Daniel O'Connell Monument and wore many hats throughout his life, as evidenced by the inscription on his statue:

Erected by public subscription to Sir John Gray Knt. MD JP, Proprietor of The Freeman's Journal; MP for Kilkenny City, Chairman of the Dublin Corporation Water Works Committee 1863 to 1875 During which period pre-eminently through his exertions the Vartry water supply was introduced to city and suburbs Born July 13 1815 Died April 9 1875.

So, he was a doctor, a journalist, an MP and, as chairman of the Dublin Corporation waterworks committee, was largely responsible for introducing fresh water supply to Dublin. Farrell depicts him holding a scroll in his left hand, in an open coat whose multiple creases suggest a carelessness, giving the impression that Sir John had more important things to focus on than his state of dress. In fact, plans were drawn up for a much bigger monument, one that evoked Ireland, with a harp and broken chains to represent such recent legislative successes as Catholic Emancipation. However, Farrell was under pressure to deliver as quickly as possible and, therefore, concentrated on the figure of John Gray.

Exchanging medicine for journalism, Gray bought the *Freeman's Journal* in 1841 and was, for a time, its political editor, declaring his support for Charles Stewart Parnell and the Irish Parliamentary Party (IPP). However, the paper's support for Parnell would not survive the Kittie O'Shea scandal and one can only wonder at Gray's own reaction had he still been alive. Founded in 1763, this was the oldest nationalist newspaper in Dublin (albeit following a pro-British phase in the mid–1780s) and, after Gray took it over, it was possibly the most popular. It makes an appearance in James Joyce's novel, *Ulysses*, as the employer of Leopold Bloom, the central character who sells ads for the paper; it also employs another fictional character in the short story 'Grace'. In his book *Modern Ireland 1600–1972*, Roy Foster refers to the *Journal* as 'the premier patriotic paper for many years'. It lasted one hundred and sixty-one years until it was merged with the *Irish Independent* in 1924.

In a 2019 article for *The Irish Times*, Felix M Larkin recounts a story told by Piaras Béaslaí (1881–1965) in the 1960s, in which he played unwitting host to James Joyce on his visit to the *Freeman*'s offices. In August 1909, Joyce was in Dublin to see a George Bernard Shaw play, having wangled a press pass for himself with the promise of reviewing the play for a Trieste newspaper. Béaslaí, a drama critic, got chatting to him and, believing he was talking to a journalist from a Trieste newspaper (he was not!), invited Joyce to visit the offices where he worked. Joyce made a lengthy visit the very next day and obviously mined all he saw and heard for chapter seven, the Aeolus episode, in *Ulysses*, where we follow Bloom into the *Freeman*'s offices.

The Vartry Scheme was formally opened on 30 June 1863. As a former doctor, this particular achievement must have been especially important to Gray because it was largely thanks to his efforts that the River Vartry, in County Wicklow, underwent redirection and damming in order to supply the city of Dublin and her suburbs with fresh water. Goodness knows how many lives were saved as a result. Up to then, the city's inhabitants, including those crammed together in squalid tenements, depended on canal water, thereby risking all manner of fatal diseases, from cholera to typhus. Yet another link with James Joyce is via John Stanislaus Joyce (1849–1931), the writer's father, who was a water rates collector for a year in 1882, his career cut short when he was found to be using the rates money for his personal gain. Today, the Vartry supplies Dublin with forty per cent of its water. Gray's scheme earned him a knighthood from the Earl of Carlisle, George William Frederick Howard (1802–1864), who was Lord Lieutenant of Ireland in 1863. Five years later, Gray declined a nomination to serve as Dublin's Lord Mayor from 1868 to 1869.

FATHER THEOBALD MATHEW

Father Mathew (1790–1856) was quite the celebrity, his popularity rivalling the likes of Daniel O'Connell and borne out by the nation's embrace of his anti-alcohol message. He toured the country, preaching against the evils of drink and inviting his listeners to sign a pledge. Approximately three million people accepted his invitation. During one five-day visit to the capital, 70,000 Dubliners took the pledge. It was a Quaker friend who

Father Theobald Mathew's statue shows him dressed as a monk, which was not his typical attire.

suggested that Father Mathew take on intemperance, resulting in the first meeting of the Cork Total Abstinence Society taking place in his Cork school house on 10 April 1838, where he declared, as he signed his name, 'Here Goes in the Name of God.' Sixty attendees signed up that first night; twelve weeks later over 25,000 names had been added.

His statue initially stood across from the Savoy Hotel but, today, it is further down O'Connell Street, almost tucked in behind the Spire.

The statue of this 'apostle of temperance', sculpted by Mary Redmond (1863–1930), was unveiled to a massive crowd on 18 February 1893. According to the *Irish Builder* trade journal in 1890, Redmond won the tender by asking for much less money than her male counterpart. It is her biggest piece of work as she mostly kept to portrait busts and medallions. Apparently, and most ironically, her model for Father Mathew arrived drunk and she sent him packing. That evening, after she had gone home, he broke into her studio near St Stephen's Green and smashed up the work in progress, forcing her to begin all over again.

In *The Buildings of Ireland: Dublin*, Christine Casey describes the Father Mathew monument as 'uninspired'. The heavy robe of the Capuchin friar is fastened in at the waist by a length of rope, from which rosary beads hang. One arm is raised whilst the other reaches out with open palm as if bestowing a blessing. Below the hem, toes peep out of sandals and the rather youthful face is a picture of serenity. However, according to the images available, he did not dress like this. His wardrobe is more aptly represented by his statue in Cork, which depicts him wearing civilian clothes. The committee behind the Dublin monument was made up of Protestants and Catholics united in a desire to have the public houses closed for the statue's unveiling.

Father Mathew did a lot more than persuade millions to avoid alcohol; he also established schools, a library, and, in 1830, he took out a lease on Dublin's Botanic Gardens in order to provide a cemetery for the poor and destitute. Plenty donated money towards his work but he gave it all away, practically bankrupting himself in 1844, in Birmingham. Unable to pay a British merchant for temperance medals, he briefly ended up in jail in October 1844; his work might have ended there, but he was rescued by Protestant and Catholic, Irish and English friends, including the prime minister Lord John Russell (1792–1878) who persuaded him to accept an annual pension of £300.

Writer Maria Edgeworth was distressed at this good man's incarceration but was relieved to read in her newspaper that Father Mathew was only guilty of 'imprudence'. Apparently, his eagerness to provide churches and so on resulted in his initiating construction work before the finances were in place. A friend of hers describes the arrest in a letter. A man presented himself to Father Mathew whilst he was doling out pledges in Chapelizod, Dublin, knelt to take the pledge and then stood up to make the arrest, before kneeling once more to beg the priest's forgiveness.

The English writer William Makepeace Thackeray (1811–1863) met

Father Mathew in Cork in 1842 and wrote that 'no man seems more eager than he for the practical improvement of his country'. This was no mean praise from a man who was appalled at the church's dominance in Ireland, both Catholic and Protestant, describing the country as 'priest-ridden'.

Amidst all the praise for Father Mathew, there is one dissenting voice. Known today as the most photographed American of the nineteenth century, former slave and abolitionist Frederick Douglass visited Ireland in August 1845. He met with Father Mathew, duly took the pledge and complimented the priest on his success. However, four years later, in 1849, Douglass was enraged when Father Mathew visited his county as part of his temperance crusade and avoided condemning slavery, which was, Douglass mused, surely as much an abomination as wanton drunkenness. Father Mathew met with President Zachary Taylor (1784–1850) and it is possible that he did not feel he was in a position to denounce slavery since the President came from a prominent plantation-owing family.

In her essay, 'Father Theobald Mathew, Apostle of Temperance', which was read to the Old Dublin Society on 9 March 1983, Moira Lysaght provides further detail about the American trip. Father Mathew arrived at Staten Island on 1 July 1849 to a tumultuous welcome. There followed lots of receptions and a banquet dinner, all duly attended by Father Mathew. However, he turned down an invitation by a group proposing to merge a temperance campaign with the need to abolish slavery. Lysaght explains Father Mathew's reluctance to get involved with the anti-slavery group as a result of his fear that he might turn a large amount of people against his temperance campaign. It hardly seems an adequate excuse.

It would appear that he believed his own campaign had to be prioritised at all costs, including that of his health. After signing up 45,000 Bostonians, Father Mathew returned to New York and collapsed, becoming so ill that he made out his will. The following week, however, saw a miraculous recovery and off he headed, to sign up thousands more in Philadelphia. He was formally recognised for his work in Washington where he was granted a seat on the US Senate floor, a privilege usually reserved for visiting English statesmen.

During his two-year American tour, Father Mathew visited twenty-five states, spoke at over 300 meetings and signed up 600,000 people. With his health precarious once more, he arrived back in Ireland on 6 December 1851, shocking his friends and supporters with his feebleness and sickly appearance.

Moira Lysaght makes reference to the book *Footprints of Fr. Mathew* by Reverend Augustine, in which she relates several accounts about Father Mathew as a healer. She particularly favours a story from 1933, seventy-seven years after Father Mathew's death, about a Corkman living in California who was losing his sight. He flew to Ireland specifically to pray over Father Mathew's grave and ask for his sight to be returned. And it was, over the next few months, allowing him to return to California with his sight fully restored.

In 2016, with the expanding of the Luas along O'Connell Street, Father Mathew's statue was removed for safekeeping, with a view to placing it elsewhere. Following discussions between Dublin City Council and the Capuchin Order concerning nineteen other possible locations, it was decided to return it to O'Connell Street.

CHARLES STEWART PARNELL

Born in Avondale, County Wicklow to a powerful Anglo-Irish Protestant family, Charles Stewart Parnell (1846–1891) was a nationalist politician, who for the last sixteen years of his life served as a member of the British parliament, during which he founded the Irish National Land League in 1879 and led a fierce campaign for Irish Home Rule; he sought to allow Ireland to run her own affairs within the constraints of the British Empire.

This monument to Charles Stewart Parnell was unveiled by MP John Redmond, 1 October 1911.

His career came to an ignominious end when his affair with a married woman, whom he subsequently married, became public.

His statue, which was unveiled by Irish MP John Redmond (1856–1918) on 1 October 1911, stands at the north end of O'Connell Street, just across from the Gate Theatre.

The sculptor of this monument, Augustus Saint-Gaudens (1848–1907), was born at 35 Charlemont Street – now the site of the Clayton Hotel – in Dublin, to an Irish mother and French father. When he was six months old, the family emigrated to America to escape the Famine.

His statues were hugely popular, including his Abraham Lincoln, America's first president, in Lincoln Park, Chicago, though many consider his masterpiece to be the hooded figure marking the grave of Marian 'Clover' Hooper Adams (1843–1885), wife of renowned intellectual Henry Adams (1838–1918), grandson and great-grandson of two American presidents. Known for her wit and intelligence, Marian read classics in their original Greek and was a successful photographer

Grief, *statue by Augustus Saint-Gaudens on the grave of Marian Hooper Adams, Rock Creek Cemetery, Washington.*

with an influential social life. Following her father's death, she struggled with depression and, on 6 December, drank potassium cyanide before rearranging herself on the rug beside the fireplace, ensuring that her husband would find her first. Henry selected the best sculptor he knew for his wife's memorial at Rock Creek Cemetery in Washington.

The Parnell monument was Saint-Gaudens' final commission and, anxious to do good by his native city, the sculptor made extensive notes in preparation, using pictures and maps of Sackville Street to work out the scale for the work. He also contacted Parnell's tailor, Phillips and Healy at 3 Dame Street, Dublin, to send him the last clothes they had made for the politician. Once he settled on his design, Saint-Gaudens built a timber copy in his studio that included a life-size figure of Parnell. He planned on coming to Dublin to see the monument launched, his first visit since leaving as a baby. However, he had been diagnosed with cancer in 1900, the same year he accepted the commission, and died three years before it was unveiled.

An article appeared in the *Irish Builder* trade journal in July 1922 complaining about how the monument obstructed traffic and that Parnell looked 'niggled and eccentric'. Cartoonist Thomas Fitzpatrick (1860–1912) depicted Parnell's ghost giving his own opinion:

Well, I never pretended to be the best-dressed man in the House of Commons; but Great Scott! I never wore trousers like these!

It is difficult today to explain these reactions. The figure of Parnell stands beside a small table, almost covered by what appears to be a grand fringed curtain or banner. With his left hand he holds fast a sheaf of papers that might otherwise fall, while his right hand is raised as if he is caught mid-speech. Historian Ronan Fitzpatrick, who gives talks about the monument, was told that locals used to joke about the fierce draught on that part of the street that obliged Parnell to wear two coats. Indeed, Parnell is wearing a long jacket and an even longer overcoat. Close inspection of the monument also reveals the bullet holes presumably sustained during the Easter Rising, the War of Independence and the Civil War.

In April 2014, a letter from Parnell to his tailor, dated 11 November 1883, went on sale at Adams Auctioneers. He was particular about the material used in his clothes. The letter is a request for a selection of Irish tweeds for a suit and, also, an order for a dress suit.

Christine Casey in her book *Buildings of Ireland*, points out how the figure of Parnell is dwarfed by the structure – the 62-foot (19-metre) wall of pink granite that bears the famous lines 'No man has the right to fix a boundary to the march of a nation ….' She also writes that this monument was the last of its kind in the Victorian tradition.

Once a powerhouse in Irish politics, Parnell died a broken man. His devoted wife Katharine (1846–1921), an English Protestant, wanted to bury him quietly in Brighton where they lived, but was told that the people of Ireland were 'entitled' to attend his funeral. And, so, she let him be taken from her for what may be the biggest Irish funeral ever. At least he had died in her arms because, in allowing him to be returned to Ireland, she knew neither she nor their three children would be buried with him.

Katharine O'Shea allowed her husband's remains to be returned to Ireland.

Approximately 200,000 mourners turned up to bid farewell to the man who was their hero until his love affair with the unhappily married Katharine was made public through her errant husband's, Captain William Henry O'Shea (1840–1905), divorce proceedings.

In 1914, Lytton Strachey, a writer and prominent member of the infamous Bloomsbury group, met the English prime minister Herbert Asquith (1852–1928), who described Parnell as the most remarkable man he had ever known.

Having led Ireland to the brink of Home Rule, Parnell finally married his 'queenie' Katherine on 25 June 1891. Three months later, ignoring his doctor's orders to rest, he sailed to Ireland to deliver a speech in Creggs, County Galway. Ignoring the bad weather, he stood in damp clothes with one arm in a sling from rheumatism, suffering from chronic exhaustion and stress. He gave a final talk in Dublin, in the rooms of the Irish National League (the nationalist party founded by Parnell after the suppression of the Irish National Land League) before boarding the ship home. Less than two weeks later he was dead, having given his all first for his country and then for the woman he loved.

Countess Daisy Fingall wrote about her school-girl fascination with Parnell in her memoir *Seventy Years Young*, mentioning his handsomeness and cultured voice. She tells how he, at his first political meeting, stood up to say something but was rendered speechless by stage fright. He was known as a haughty man, but the countess defends this as typical of anyone who had only one great passion in their lives, such as his for Ireland. Out walking one day with Thomas Patrick 'TP' Gill (1858–1931) of the Irish Parliamentary Party, the countess spied Parnell coming out of Morrison's Hotel. Gill called to Parnell and introduced the countess as an admirer. Parnell looked unconvinced as she represented the class who hated him most. His coldness made her stumble her words, 'I know, Mr Parnell, that you really love Ireland.' His response was instant, the aloofness gone,

Elizabeth, Countess of Fingall, whose memoirs provide an extraordinary insight into nineteenth-century Ireland.

replaced by the warmest of smiles and he even took her hand.

He was buried on 11 October 1891, a day that began with heavy rain which was replaced with sunshine by early afternoon. The huge funeral cortège included an old horse called *Home Rule* and finally reached Glasnevin at 5.30pm, needing police officers to help get through the dense crowds. Astronomy being one of his few interests outside politics, Parnell would have appreciated what happened next. Amidst the tears and laments, witnesses, including revolutionary and long-time muse for WB Yeats Maud Gonne (1866–1953), writer and historian Standish O'Grady (1846–1928) and poet James Stephens (1880–1950), saw a bright light – a meteor – shoot across the evening sky, as if the heavens also wanted to mark his passing.

JAMES LARKIN

Born in Liverpool to Irish parents, James Larkin (1876–1947), known as Big Jim Larkin, was a key figure in the republican movement and an ardent socialist, trade unionist and a champion of the Irish worker. The dynamic pose of Larkin's statue, which stands in front of Clery's, is an iconic one

June 1979, officiated by President Patrick Hillery, the unveiling of James Larkin's statue, depicting the man in his characteristic dynamic pose.

that took its inspiration from a photograph by Joseph Cashman (1881–1969), showing James Larkin addressing a crowd on O'Connell Street. All we notice in the photograph is Larkin. Towering over everyone else, he is totally given over to the delivery of his message. The large mouth is wide open, oval-shaped as if in song, with both arms reaching towards the sky, barely contained by the billowing jacket that bunches up at his shoulders. It is quite a pose, one that shows off Larkin as a figure of physical strength and power whilst also suggesting a vulnerability; he was just a man after all. The group of men and boys immediately around him do not appear to be paying him any attention. This is not 1913 but ten years later, after Larkin's return from America. It is best to ignore those who seem distracted, which sculptor Oisín Kelly does when recreating Larkin's stance for his 21-foot (6.4-metre) bronze statue.

Dubliner Kelly, a former teacher, was a popular choice thanks to his

Children of Lir monument for Dublin's Garden of Remembrance, which was unveiled by President Éamon de Valera on Easter Monday, in 1966, for the fiftieth anniversary of Easter 1916.

Commissioned by the General Executive Committee of the Workers' Union of Ireland, Kelly began working on a plaster figure of Larkin in his back garden in Firhouse, using his neighbour, actor Eddie Golden (1912–1983), as his model. The plaster Larkin was then cast in bronze at the Dublin Art Foundry. It stands atop a large pedestal which, to the front, is engraved with Larkin's most famous slogan in French, Irish and English:

The great appear great because we are on our knees. Let us rise!

This quote did not originate with Larkin. He is probably quoting the French revolutionist Camille Desmoulins (1760–1794) who was beheaded on 2 April 1794.

On the west side of the base are lines from Patrick Kavanagh's poem, 'Jim Larkin', first published in 1947:

And Tyranny trampled them in Dublin's gutter
Until Jim Larkin came along and cried
The call of Freedom and the call of Pride
And Slavery crept to its hands and knees
And Nineteen Thirteen cheered from out the utter
Degradation of their miseries.

The text on the east side is taken from *Drums under the Windows*, the third volume of Seán O'Casey's autobiography, published in 1945:

… He talked to the workers, spoke as only Jim Larkin could speak, not for an assignation with peace, dark obedience, or placed resignation, but trumpet-tongued of resistance to wrong, discontent with leering poverty, and defiance of any power strutting out to stand in the way of their march onward.

The Larkin statue does not hold a scroll or a sheaf of papers, unlike most of its counterparts throughout O'Connell Street. This figure is much too busy to realise that he is being captured by the photographer and then by the sculptor. However, the best of our poets and the writers provide us with all the information that we need to understand the legend that was Larkin and why his statue was a worthy addition alongside the likes of Gray and O'Connell.

President Patrick Hillery (1923–2008) unveiled the work on 15 June 1979, to the applause of several hundred onlookers and invited guests. It was an occasion of note as this was the first twentieth-century monument, since Parnell's in 1911, to commemorate an individual on O'Connell Street. Indeed, the President made the point that:

It is not often in the history of a capital city that the occasion arises for the unveiling of a monument in its principal thoroughfare.

There was a slight hiccup regarding his date of birth as Larkin put it about that he was two years younger than he was. Thanks to historian C Desmond Graves, who found Larkin's birth certificate in Liverpool in 1980, we know now that he was born in 1874 and not 1876.

The statue was ready in 1978 but was delayed by two years due to the prolonged search for a stone big enough for the pedestal. Larkin's son Denis preferred that the pedestal be cut out of one stone but this proved impossible.

The location of the statue is hugely relevant as it stands in front of Clery's Department Store, formerly the Imperial Hotel, which was owned by Larkin's greatest enemy – the Irish businessman, press baron and politician William Martin Murphy (1845–1919). Larkin chose the hotel's balcony to address his followers on that infamous Sunday in August 1913 during the Dublin Lockout, blatantly defying his police ban.

A year after the unveiling, RTÉ ran a seven-part adaptation of Joseph Plunkett's (1920–2003) bestselling novel *Strumpet City* (published 1963), set during the 1913 Lockout. The Larkin statue provided a challenge for the cameramen as its location meant a constant battle, during the re-enacted 1913 riots, to ensure that it could not be seen. Denis Larkin was photographed at home by an *Irish Press* photographer, watching the series with a small replica of the statue sitting by the television.

THE SPIRE OF DUBLIN

A five-minute amateur video on YouTube shows a thronged O'Connell Street on Tuesday, 21 January 2003. Thanks to Eason's clock, we can see that it is after midday when the eighth and final section of the Spire is put in place. Two men wearing hard hats are standing inside the tube to accept the last piece that dangles from a massive crane. Gradually, they disappear from sight as they encase themselves inside. The top is barely in place before the crowd cheers and applauds such a precarious-looking feat. One of the onlookers was seventy-year-old Liam Sutcliffe, who took a special interest in the new monument, having been responsible for the destruction of Nelson's Pillar that had stood there previously.

Commissioned by Dublin Corporation, the 393 feet (120 metres) of stainless steel was the winning design of an architect competition to finally replace Nelson's Pillar that was blown up by Sutcliffe in 1966. The winner, out of the 205 entries, was Ian Ritchie Architects, a London-based firm. This was the brief:

The Spire was not everyone's favourite choice for O'Connell Street.

> The monument shall have a vertical emphasis, an elegant structure of twenty-first century contemporary design which shall relate to the quality and scale of O'Connell Street as represented by the late eighteenth- and early twentieth-century architecture.

It is a monument without text; however, the pattern on its base can be read, according to its architect, as a sea or lake that glistens with hundreds of islands.

Historian Donal Fallon, in an article for *The Journal.ie*, explained why it took thirty-seven years to replace Nelson's Pillar. Previous ideas included the reconstruction of the Pillar for a statue of James Joyce. One particularly attractive suggestion was a Millennium Arch, on which would sit a sculpted eternal flame to represent the city's undying spirit.

Several hated the idea of the Spire or, as it was originally known, the 'Monument of Light'. One of its more flamboyant critics was the artist

Micheál Ó Nualláin (1928–2016), brother of Brian O'Nolan – the writer Flann O'Brien/Myles na Gopaleen (1911–66). Ó Nualláin had submitted his own intriguing idea – a sort of flying saucer comprising of a 'skypod' that would sit atop a six-sided column which, in turn, would jut out of a three-storey box on the street. A work, he declared, that would provoke the same initial shocked response that greeted Paris's Eiffel Tower on its completion in 1889. Potential embellishments included a revolving restaurant in the skypod and underground toilets that could house flowers and plants. Furthermore, the entire monument was to symbolise the legendary CuChulainn, the skypod his shield and the tower his sword.

In fact, Ó Nualláin went so far as to initiate legal action against Dublin Corporation to prevent the Spire being built, his affidavit citing that it clashed with the history and architecture on O'Connell Street. He also argued for the necessity of an Environmental Impact Statement (EIS) and in this he was successful. In July 1999, the court ruled that an EIS was required before the spire could be built which delayed its construction.

ANNA LIVIA PLURABELLE

Succeeded by the Spire, in 1988, was the *Anna Livia Plurabelle* monument, a fountain that was – briefly – the only female representation to grace O'Connell Street. Commissioned by businessman Michael Smurfit in memory of his father, this was the work of renowned Derry sculptor Éamonn O'Doherty (1939–2011). The statue of the tall, slim and naked reclining woman, with long tangled hair, was based on the character Anna Livia Plurabelle from *Finnegans Wake*, James Joyce's final novel (published 1939). She was both woman and Dublin's River Liffey. Novelist Edna O'Brien (*b.* 1930), writing in *The Guardian*, concluded that Anna Livia Plurabelle was not an inspirational heroine like Gustav Flaubert's Emma Bovary or Daniel Defoe's Moll Flanders. Rather, she was the sum total of

Joyce's numerous woes at this time: his dwindling health and popularity, his beloved daughter's admittance into an asylum and, not least, the warning growls of another world war. O'Brien refers to Anna Livia as Joyce's final creation and, therefore, his 'farewell to words'.

Both her long reddish hair and her name were 'borrowed' from Livia Svevo (1896–1928), the wife of Joyce's friend and novelist Italo Svevo (1861–1928). Richard Ellman interviewed her for his biography of Joyce, and she told him that while she had been flattered to have her hair represent Dublin's Liffey, she was disgusted that Joyce placed two washerwomen in the river to wash dirty linen.

In the novel, Joyce has Anna Livia call out, 'Is there one who understands me?' This cry for help is also appropriate for O'Doherty's statue. Acknowledging that there were not many places on O'Connell Street to

rest, O'Doherty wanted to provide enough space for two hundred people to sit and enjoy his work and, quite quickly, that was the case. During the summer, she was a welcome spot for weary shoppers and tourists, although one had to strain to hear the running water over the deluge of traffic noise. She had her detractors and ignoble

Livia Svevo, whose hair was the inspiration for James Joyce's character Anna Livia Plurabelle.

nicknames – the 'Floozie in the Jacuzzi' and the 'Hoor in the Sewer' to mention just two – but ultimately Dubliners accepted her presence. Unfortunately, the low wall that surrounded her attracted not just the shoppers and young families but also others who were not so welcome. Where else on O'Connell Street could you sit and enjoy several cans of beer alfresco of an afternoon? And where else could you dump those empty cans or used needles or fast food packaging? The fountain's beauty was marred by the evidence of the darker appetites of a capital city. Michael Smurfit received a letter from a concerned citizen telling him that the fountain should be made to disappear as it no longer served as a worthy memorial to his father nor as an enhancement to O'Connell Street.

The running water was switched off and, in November 2001, the fountain was removed to a holding location until a new venue could be found. Following a decade spent inside a crate in Raheny, and some refurbishment, she was floated down the Liffey in 2011 to her new home. Today, the statue of *Anna Livia Plurabelle* seemingly hovers above the pond in Croppies Memorial Park, which is dedicated to those who died in the 1798 Rebellion, near Heuston Station on Wolfe Tone Quay.

JAMES JOYCE

This 8-foot (almost 2-and-a-half-metre) bronze statue of Dublin's famous writer, James Joyce (1882–1941), described as 'kitsch' by Christine Casey, in her book *Buildings of Ireland*, stands at the junction of O'Connell Street and Talbot Street. It was commissioned by the

The statue of writer James Joyce by the American-born sculptor Marjorie Fitzgibbon.

North Earl Street Business Association and The Dublin City Centre Business Association – spearheaded by Arthur Walls, then chairman of Clery's – to celebrate the pedestrianisation of the side streets around O'Connell Street. Walls may have been a distant relative of James Joyce, who proved a popular subject with the association. His popularity was partly to do with his place in Irish literature but also due to the Association wishing to acknowledge the writer as a fellow neighbourhood businessman. Joyce had completed a three-month stint as an entrepreneur in the entertainment industry.

On 20 December 1909, Joyce launched Ireland's first cinema, the Volta, at 45 Mary Street (now Penneys) in the belief that he would make his fortune from it. He and his family were living in Trieste, where he was a frequent cinema-goer. Influenced by the profits made by two theatres there, he convinced their owners and two others to back his venture, telling them about Dublin with its population of 500,000 and not one cinema. Academics argue about how much he was driven by economics versus genuinely wanting to bring broader international culture to his native city. Certainly, he wanted to show the sort of films that proved popular with the Italians and French, especially those that he particularly he enjoyed himself as an opera fan.

Fifteen-year-old Frank Duff whiled away many an afternoon in the Volta when he should have been in school. Joyce gave the boy a permanent pass and they watched films together, to the soundtrack of the Guinness-tippling pianist. It was a beautiful dream that did not last, Joyce's backers quit and the cinema was sold in June 1910 after Dubliners failed to be interested in its European fare.

American-born artist and sculptor Marjorie Fitzgibbon (1930–2018) specialised in bronze statues and was asked to submit an idea for a statue of Joyce. When her maquette proved an instant hit with the committee, she took just ten months to complete the life-size model, at the cost of IR£20,000. Fitzgibbon led an interesting and varied life. At seventeen, she left the family home in Nevada in her quest to become a Hollywood actress. Two years later, she married Huntington Hartford (1911–2008), the thirty-six-year-old multimillionaire heir to the A&P supermarket chain. She divorced him after seven years and married the English actor Dudley Sutton (1933–2018), best known for his part in the TV series *Lovejoy*. That marriage was drenched in alcohol and lasted just four years before she met her final husband, Constantine Fitzgibbon (1919–1983), at a drying-out clinic. Constantine, an American-born Irish writer and historian, had been previously married to Irish food writer, model and actress Theodora Rosling (1916–1991). Marjorie and Constantine married in 1967, honeymooning in Greece, where Marjorie fell in love with sculpture. On arriving in Ireland, she set about teaching herself to sculpt and eighteen months later had her first exhibit at the Brown Thomas Gallery.

It proved a productive marriage for the both of them until Constantine's death from cancer. He wrote several books, while her talent soared in popularity. Initially settling in Bantry in 1967, Marjorie was happier when they moved to Dublin. Her works include a bust of Pope John Paul II and Steven Hawking as well as twelve bronze heads of prominent Irish writers, from Seamus Heaney to Jonathan Swift, housed in the library of the RDS (Royal Dublin Society).

PATRICK SHEAHAN

Designed by William Patrick O'Neill (1856?–1957?), this monument of Patrick Sheahan (1876–1905), which sits nearby on Hawkins Street, was commissioned by the Mansion House Committee in 1906 to commemorate a true hero. Instead of a statue there is a Celtic cross atop a limestone ornate block. The explicit inscription compensates for the absence of a figure. From the monument we do not know what Sheahan looked like but we know exactly why we should remember him.

A monument to the brave constable Patrick Sheahan.

73

Twenty-nine-year-old Constable Patrick Sheahan, a Limerick man, died in an attempt to rescue three Corporation workmen who had been overcome by gas. However, even before this Sheahan had proved his fearlessness. Weighing in at 18 stone (114 kilograms), with a 6-foot-4-inch (193-centimetre) frame, he was well equipped to cope with such challenges as rescuing an elderly couple from a collapsing building in Townsend Street and wrestling a runaway bull into submission on Grafton Street. The bull was being herded along Harcourt Street on Wednesday, 23 March 1904 when it made a run for it, knocking over some unlucky pedestrians – including a five-year-old boy – before arriving onto a busy Grafton Street. Sheahan and a colleague, along with a stableman, followed the animal into Anne's Lane and somehow got a rope around its neck, forcing it to the ground.

Sheahan also retrieved an Irish flag from a group of Trinity College students in Dawson Street and returned it to its rightful place in the Mansion House, for which he received an award.

The Limerick Chronicle devoted a double-page spread to what then happened on Saturday, 6 May 1905. At 3pm, John Fleming opened up a manhole at the corner of Hawkins Street and Burgh Quay and descended 24 feet (7 metres) into the sewer to check out a broken pipe but found himself immediately in peril from gas. A newspaper boy rushed to get help, summoning Constable Sheahan from his position at O'Connell Bridge. More than likely Fleming was already dead when Sheahan went down the ladder before he too succumbed to the fumes. Two others had followed Sheahan's descent and were also overcome by the gas. A hackney-driver, Kevin Fitzpatrick, tied a rope around his waist and lowered himself into the hole, managing to pull out the last two men in time, thus saving their lives. Sheahan was a bachelor, while Fleming left a widow and nine children, the youngest only a few months old.

The constable's early morning funeral mass was held in Mount Argus the following Tuesday. Afterwards, the cortège, following the mounted division of the Dublin Metropolitan Police and accompanied by bands from the DMP and RIC (Royal Irish Constabulary), made its way to Kingsbridge Railway Station, along streets lined with mourners that had turned out to bid a brave man farewell. The coffin was placed on the 9.15am Limerick train which was met by Sheahan's devastated mother.

That August, a public subscription was opened for a memorial to Sheahan and Fleming. Lord Aberdeen (John Campbell Gordon 1847–1934) who was lord lieutenant of Ireland at that time, led by example, pledging £25. A year later, in August 1906, the monument was unveiled by the Lord Mayor of Dublin, Joseph Hutchison.

Ten years would pass before the next DMP death, also the first casualty of the 1916 Rising: Constable James O'Brien (1868–1916), who was shot dead by Seán Connolly, (1882–1916).

Sheahan's great-nephew is the composer and musician John Sheahan (b. 1939), who is the last surviving member of the original line-up of the hugely successful group The Dubliners. Sheahan retired the group in 2012, on their fiftieth anniversary, following the death of founding member Barry McKenna (b. 1939).

NELSON'S PILLAR

Originally from Norfolk, Horatio Nelson (1758–1805) joined the Royal Navy as a twelve-year-old in 1770. He was made a captain eight years later and from there worked his way up the ranks, finally being promoted to Vice Admiral in 1803, and taking charge of the navy's Mediterranean fleet. On 21 October, he led his twenty-seven ships into battle against a combined force of thirty-three Spanish and French ships. The Battle of Trafalgar was a resounding British success thanks to the Vice Admiral's confidence in his men and his utter fearlessness.

The monument that divided generations of Irishmen and women.

From 1808 to 1966, Nelson's Pillar stood in the centre of O'Connell Street, where the Spire stands today.

At 1.32am on Tuesday, 8 March 1966, the explosion must have been mighty when a bomb blew the top off of Nelson's Pillar, sending it crashing into the street – an era shattered in an instant. It is nothing short of a miracle that no one was hurt, especially considering that a night of dancing at the Metropole Ballroom had just ended, its patrons emerging to make their way home.

Nelson's death at the Battle of Trafalgar prompted James Vance, Dublin's Lord Mayor in 1805, to suggest a public commemoration of Admiral Horatio Nelson's successes. Despite the fact that Nelson had no personal connection with Ireland, it proved a popular proposal with Dublin's elite – bankers, nobility, clergy and merchants, including Arthur Guinness junior, stepped up to fund the creation of a monument, donating a total of £5,000. It is believed that they wanted to acknowledge his making the seas safer for merchant ships and businessmen.

The initial architect, Londoner William Wilkins (1778–1839), submitted an overly expensive plan that included a Roman galley at the top of the Pillar. He was replaced by Irish architect Francis Johnston (1760–1829), who modified Wilkins's design to the more affordable 134–foot (40.84-metre) Doric column on which stood a 13-foot (3.96-metre) statue of Nelson, minus a right arm and a right eye, sculpted by Corkman Thomas Kirk (1781–1845). Johnston was also the architect behind the General Post Office (GPO) on O'Connell Street; Nelson's Pillar and the GPO building formed a grand vista. Johnston's two creations would come to symbolise Dublin in the mid-nineteenth century.

Initially, debate ensued as to where to place the monument, with the Wide Streets Commissioners suggesting somewhere along the River Liffey as an appropriate location, where it could be seen by sailors. However, this suggestion may have been influenced by Sackville Street's affluent residents who worried that the new monument would draw crowds of noisy visitors and disrupt their peace. It ended up on Sackville Street, allegedly thanks to Lord Lieutenant Charles Lennox (4th Duke of Richmond) (1764–1819) who had favoured this location.

The dud eye and missing arm were just two of a lengthy list of ills that plagued the man. Ironically, the Admiral suffered from seasickness all his life. He also contracted, at various stages, malaria, dysentery, yellow fever, poisoning, scurvy, blinding headaches, indigestion, palpitations and, not

Nelson's Pillar was designed to complement the General Post Office by Francis Johnston (1760–1829).

too surprisingly, depression. His face would have appeared somewhat collapsed owing to the number of teeth he had lost to scurvy. He thought himself near death several times but always managed to soldier on until that final injury during the Battle of Trafalgar. At 1pm, or thereabouts, on 21 October 1805, he was shot through the shoulder and spine. Once again, he announced to his men, 'I have but a short time to live.' However, this time he was right and he died at approximately 4.30pm.

The foundation stone was laid on 15 February 1808 with much pomp and ceremony, the procession of dignitaries including Fellows and the Provost of Trinity College, along with the lord lieutenant and his wife, Lady Charlotte Gordon (1768–1842) dressed in mourning clothes. Nelson had attended their parties at their Brussels residence. The monument was completed in August 1809 and opened two months later, when for ten pence one could climb the 168 steps to the top of the column for a breathtaking view of the city. Nelson's Pillar gradually slotted into the city's everyday life, becoming a busy terminus for most of the tram routes; the first trams arrived from Donnybrook and Clontarf at 6am, with the last trams of the day leaving the Pillar between 11 and 11.40pm.

Maria Edgeworth describes a visit to Dublin, in October 1812, to see English balloonist James Sadler (1753–1828) make the first attempt to fly across the Irish Sea. There was great excitement with people travelling from all over to witness the massive balloon. Naturally, the weather toyed with everyone's emotions, but finally, on Thursday, 1 October, the conditions were

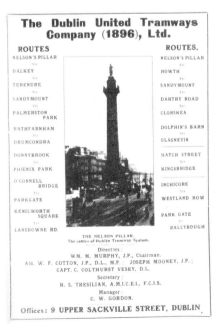

Dublin United Tramways Company poster, 1896.

perfect and the breaking news – that Sadler would fly – was conveyed by a flag flown from Nelson's Pillar. Huge crowds made their way to Belvedere House, near Drumcondra, to watch Sadler's ascent into the sky. It ended in near disaster with Sadler narrowly escaping death by drowning.

Queen Victoria made the first of four state visits to Dublin in August 1849, the first royal visit since King George IV's in 1821. It was just a couple of short years after the Famine, during which she had contributed £2,000 towards relieving Ireland's hunger. Dublin put its best foot forward and somehow, amid the squalor, a cholera breakout, the rundown buildings with broken windows and the empty shops long out of business and so on, the Queen and her family were impressed with what they were shown.

A particular highlight was the lighting show on Sackville Street. Thanks to Trinity College's Professor Gluckman, the GPO was lit up by two beams of electric light being shone from the top of Nelson's Pillar. By this stage quite a few Dubliners were fans of the monument, calling it 'Dublin's Glory'.

In the third volume of his memoir, *Drums Under the Window*, playwright Seán O'Casey (1880–1964) describes his first encounter with a George Bernard Shaw play. On a friend's recommendation, he buys a sixpence edition of *John Bull's Other Island* and starts reading it before his evening shift for the Gaelic League. He misses his shift, finding himself unable to close the book until he had finished it. His passion ignited, the next day he sees Shaw everywhere he goes, even seeing him standing on top of that huge Doric column instead of Nelson, 'with a questioning smile on his roguish face'.

Later on, O'Casey imagines a row breaking out between Nelson and Saint Patrick who tells him, 'if all had their rights, me bucko, it's not you'd be stuck up there in a state of honour, but me …'.

Nelson was not a popular figure for everyone and there were plenty of proposals down the years to have the monument dismantled and moved elsewhere. In 1853, new plans were drawn up for Dublin and, as far as *The Irish Builder* magazine was concerned, the only decent plan referred to removing Nelson from his Sackville Street perch. Over twenty years later, in 1876, Dublin City Corporation considered moving it before discovering that to do so was illegal because the monument belonged to its trustees and, therefore, any change would have required an Act of the Oireachtas.

Prince Napoléon Joseph Charles Paul Bonaparte (1822–91), first cousin of the Emperor Napoléon III, Nelson's great nemesis, arrived in Dublin by yacht on Monday, 31 July 1865, for a discreet stopover. He visited the Dublin International Exhibition in Earlsfort Terrace on arrival and on the following day went to the Zoo. He also did some shopping in College Green and perhaps had no time to climb up to Nelson's viewing platform, should he have wanted to.

Critics of the Pillar claimed that it was an eyesore that hindered traffic and blocked light from the streets around it. In 1881, the businessmen got involved, for the sake of improving the efficiency of their deliveries, sponsoring a bill in Westminster to move Nelson to Parnell's spot. This sparked much controversy, with loud mutterings about moving the statues of the dead to make way for the living. In 1923, the Dublin Citizens' Association voted to get rid of the monument. The poet and writer William Butler Yeats noted how it dwarfed the Parnell statue, by far the more interesting of the two.

Further protests and proposals were made but in vain. At one point the Arts Council defended it, pointing out that Nelson was standing on 'the finest example of a Doric column in existence'.

So, the admiral's statue and its single eye beheld the 1913 Lockout riots, the fires of the 1916 Rising, the War of Independence and the Civil War. In fact, when the first of the infernos erupted during Easter week at the Cable Shoe Company on Sackville Street, it was the Pillar's fire bell that raised the first alarm. Over the years, it became an obvious meeting point for Dubliners and tourists alike and plenty scaled the steps to take in the city's landscape from its viewing platform.

In the 1950s, German writer Heinrich Böll (1917–1985) published *Irish Journal*, a gently humorous account of his family's visit to Ireland. They find themselves in the city before ten in the morning and Böll remarks that it was the only time that he found the locals unhelpful, as anyone he asks for help merely replies with a terse 'sorry', otherwise he might have asked for the identity of the tall figure protruding through the morning's mist. By the time he realises that it is Nelson, he buys a local paper, *The Irish Digest*, to read with his breakfast. The first item he sees is a letter demanding that Nelson's statue be torn down and replaced by the Virgin Mary.

Meanwhile, other imperial works were done away with, like the statue of King William at College Green that was blown up in 1929. It is remarkable that Nelson's Pillar lasted until 1966, almost making it to the fiftieth anniversary of the Rising. Perhaps its longevity was due to its status as a city-centre terminus or the fact that the figure of Nelson was so high over everyone's heads, where it was easily ignored. Most Dubliners simply called it 'The Pillar'.

In March 1961, the broadcaster Alan Whicker (1921–2013) presented his popular programme, *Whicker's World*, from O'Connell Street, introducing his British audience to the street's statues in memory of Irish heroes, the giants of Ireland's past, before feigning surprise as he cries out, 'Nelson? What are you doing here?'

A woman, it seems, was to blame for the Pillar's demise. In an interview with the BBC, former IRA member Liam Sutcliffe (1933–2017) repeated the taunting of a Belfast girl who asked him outright what he was going to do about the British admiral lording it over the city. It occurred to him that destroying the monument would be a fine way to commemorate the fiftieth anniversary of the Easter Rising.

What he did was bring a bomb and his three-year-old son, who would innocently provide his cover as that of a typical sightseer. The bomb failed to detonate. It must have been an alarming experience to return to the Pillar the following morning, as soon as it opened, to collect the unexploded bomb. He brought it back a week later on 7 March, having tweaked its timer. Last to leave, he bid the caretaker a good evening and went home.

The end of an era and a miracle that there were no casualties.

Unbelievably, he went to bed and slept the night through. The next morning, he bumped into a woman he knew who asked him if he had heard about the Pillar. Boarding a bus for work, he read what had happened in the newspapers over the shoulders of his fellow passengers and professed his gratitude that the bomb had done its job and there were no fatalities.

The government promptly decided that the rest of the Pillar should be blown up too. Sutcliffe felt that Taoiseach Seán Lemass (1899–1971) and Frank Aiken (1898–1983), Tánaiste and Minister for External Affairs, both of whom had been in the IRA and had fought for the War of Independence, were indulging themselves at Nelson's expense since a wrecking ball would have worked just as well. And, so it was, on 14 March 1966, a crowd convened on O'Connell Street to watch the army demolish the rest of the Pillar with a controlled explosion. You can watch the footage online although the cheers of the onlookers cannot be heard. Matthew Byrne, in his book *Dublin and Her People*, writes that the only broken window following the army's work was the one left open by Radio Éireann staff above the GPO. Online footage, however, shows a few shattered shop windows.

The head of the statue was removed to a storage yard from where, ten days later, it embarked on its own journey when it was stolen by a group of enterprising NCAD (National College of Art and Design) students who saw an opportunity to pay off their debts. Ken Dolan, one of the students, was interviewed by the BBC in 2005. They made good money from 'renting' out the head for events. It appeared on stage at the Olympia with The Dubliners and on the sleeve of *Freedom's Sons*, a Clancy Brothers and Tommy Makem album. It also featured in a few television advertisements, including a photo shoot for ladies' stockings, and Lord knows how many parties it attended as a celebrity curio piece. It proved a worthwhile investment for the students whose only problem was the gardaí that were in hot pursuit of the stolen goods. Feeling the heat, they brought the head overseas to an art dealer's shop in London, where the owner, Benny Gray, paid them

The head of Nelson's statue can be found in Pearse Street Library, which is presumably its final resting place.

£250 a month to display it in his window. The fun ended when some innocent students were rounded up by the Gardaí. Gray returned the head to Ireland, driving it up O'Connell Street on a lorry for all to see and stopping to ask if anyone at all would accept it on behalf of Dublin Corporation. Today, the head sits in a display case in Pearse Street Library.

The year before his death, Senator Owen Sheehy-Skeffington (1909–70), son of murdered nationalist Francis, lamented on the absence of the Pillar. The senator was adamant that it could and should have been repaired. He felt that the city has lost something precious in the bombing of the monument and now Dublin looked like any other city. And here is writer and surgeon Oliver St John Gogarty's poetic description of it, from his 1937 memoir *As I Was Going Down Sackville Street*:

> I gazed up Sackville Street. The grandest thing we have in Dublin, the great Doric column that upheld the Admiral, was darkened by flying mists, intermittent as battle smoke; but aloft in light, silvery as the moonshine of legend, the statue in whiter stone gazed for ever southwards towards Trafalgar and the Nile.

In 1969, the Nelson Pillar Act was passed whereby the trustees were financially compensated for both the loss of the Pillar and the loss of its admission fees. However, it must be said the Pillar proved a grand money-making machine for scores of local youngsters who collected its bits and crumbs to sell door to door. At the time keeping goldfish was *en vogue*. The fish were sold at Uncle George's Pet Shop on Marlborough Street, although it was best to bring your own jam jar as this was before plastic bags. Uncle George's was a delight for children thanks largely to the infamous Jacko, a Mynah bird, who told customers to 'feck off!' Glistening chunks of Nelson's pillar were fashionable décor for any proud fish tank owner.

DEATH OF CÚ CHULAINN

Originally from Cookstown in County Tyrone, sculptor Oliver Sheppard (1865–1941) spent most of his life in Dublin. He completed the plaster model of this statue of the legendary hero as early as 1911 and, three years later, exhibited it at the Royal Hibernian Academy. After that, it lay in his

Oliver Sheppard's statue depicts the legendary Cú Chulainn in his final moments.

studio until the early 1930s when it was chosen by President Éamon de Valera (1882–1975) to be the official state memorial to the 1916 Rising, and cast in bronze in Brussels by the *Compagnie des Bronzes*.

The dying Cú Chulainn is Sheppard's most iconic piece and was partly inspired by *Cuchulain of Muirthemne*, Lady Augusta Gregory's (1852–1932) translation of the Cú Chulainn myth which was published in 1902. In her 2011 biography of the playwright, *Lady Gregory: An Irish Life*, Judith Hill quotes Gregory's diary, where she relates a dream in which her friend William Butler Yeats tells her that her job as a writer was to create an atmosphere.

Gregory was inspired, in turn, by Thomas Malory's (*c*. 1415–71) interpretation of the tales of King Arthur and the Knights of the Round Table, *Le Morte d'Arthur* (*The Death of Arthur*), first published in 1485. She wished to write about the legendary powerful, prehistoric Ulster race that included the superhero warrior Cú Chulainn, who is blinded by his rage to the point where he struggles to discern friend from foe. His glorious life is cut short in County Louth when he is confronted by numerous lifelong foes, mostly avenging sons whose fathers he had killed. After being fatally wounded by his own spear, he begs the avengers for a sip of water from a nearby lake, where stands a tall pillar-like rock that was a marker for the grave of some ancient hero. To outwit his would-be killers, Cú Chulainn tied himself to it in order to remain standing as he died. It worked. His enemies watched him for three days and dared not approach until a raven landed on his shoulder without provoking a response. The raven was Morrigan, the goddess of war and fertility, who proved that Cú Chulainn was finally no more.

The statue was placed in the window of the GPO at the end of 1934 and unveiled the following year on Easter Sunday, 21 April. Paula Murphy, in her essay '1916 Centenary: Warriors and Statemen' for *Irish Arts Review*, pointed out that Sheppard was not political and had taken no part in the Rising. His work stemmed from culture, not politics, although he was quoted in *The Irish Press* affirming that Ireland 'should be a free country'. She also asked why de Valera did not wait until the following year to unveil the statue. Surely the twentieth anniversary made more sense to commemorate than the nineteenth. However, as the most senior survivor of the Rising, it was the President's right to mark how and whenever he liked and he chose the dying Ulsterman to represent Pádraig Pearse and his comrades dying for Ireland.

Oliver St John Gogarty also used Cú Chulainn to discuss his idea of the modern Irish hero. He believed that Dan Breen (1894–1969), the politician that was involved with the first fatal ambush of the War of Independence, was a modern personification of Cú Chulainn.

William Butler Yeats wrote 'The Statues', one of his last poems, in 1938. Inspired by Sheppard's work, the last verse begins:

When Pearse summoned Cuchulainn to his side,
What walked through the Post Office?

FIDELITY, HIBERNIA AND MERCURY

Three statues sit on the portico of the GPO: *Fidelity*, *Hibernia* and *Mercury*. Mercury is the Roman god of circulation, that is the movement of goods and people. He was also believed to protect shopkeepers and, as a gifted mediator, he became chief messenger to the gods. Harp in hand, the central figure Hibernia is Ireland, personified in the classical female form, while Fidelity, with her faithful hound at her feet and a key in her right hand, represents the trust placed in our national postal service. They were sculpted by John Smyth (*c*. 1773–1840) in 1814. Smyth received his training at Dublin Society's Drawing School before following his father Edward (1749–1812), famous as the sculptor of the Riverine Gods on Custom House, into the family business based at 36 Montgomery Street (now Foley Street).

The GPO statues survived the fires of the Easter 1916 Rising.

According to the 1913 *A Dictionary of Irish Arts*, John's work was inferior to that of his father's.

In his 1890 guide to Ireland, the writer William F Wakeman (1822–1900) reproduces a conversation that took place between a tourist and a jarvey, a driver of a small horse and carriage. As they passed the GPO in the rain, the tourist, noting the three grand statues on its roof, asked his driver who they were. Not wanting to lose face, the cabby declared them to be the twelve apostles. On questioning this explanation from a number's perspective, the tourist was told that in bad weather the apostles only came out three at a time.

Apart from the GPO statues, John received the contract to repair the statue of William III when it was blown up in 1836, the explosion sending the figure of the victor of the 1690 Battle of the Boyne several feet into the air and causing a man nearby to have a fatal heart attack. Two prostitutes had watched the bomber set his charge and light the fuse but no arrests were ever made.

The GPO statues were never more striking than after the Rising when the post office was in ruins, its roof and interior in ashes on the ground. Somehow, the trio survived the gunboat shelling and the ensuing fires and remained steadfast up until the 1970s when it was decided to replace them.

The founders of the Gate Theatre, Hilton Edwards and Micheál MacLiammóir.

CHAPTER THREE

Landmark Buildings

THE GATE THEATRE (NEARBY O'CONNELL STREET)

The building first opened its doors in 1784 as the New Assembly Rooms, an extension of the Rotunda Hospital. Originally known as the Rotunda Hall, where John Henry Newman (later to be Cardinal Newman) delivered his 1851 series of lectures entitled 'The Idea of a University', the theatre finally came into being in 1928 thanks to the acclaimed actors and life partners Micheál MacLiammóir (1899–1978) and Hilton Edwards (1903–82). Together they were known as 'The Boys', and were probably Ireland's first openly homosexual couple.

MacLiammóir's fascinating memoir *Enter a Goldfish* is 224 pages in length and The Gate is finally mentioned on page 222 as a newly established theatre on the northside that would provide Dublin with an international programme. Its first performance actually took place in the Peacock Theatre in October 1928, with the Norwegian play *Peer Gynt*, where, following a successful first season, the theatre relocated to the Rotunda.

The actual company – Dublin Gate Theatre Company Ltd – was

established on Christmas Eve, 1929, with five directors, including its two founders, and £2,500 that was available in one pound shares, although not all of these were sold.

Six weeks later, on 17 February, there was a grand opening for Goethe's *Faust*, the tragic play about an intellectual who is so bored with his life that he offers the devil his soul in exchange for unlimited knowledge and worldly pleasures. Hilton Edwards took the starring role with MacLiammóir playing Mephistopheles, the devil's representative who strikes the deal with Faust.

One imagines that nerves must have blazed as not only was the play on trial that first night, but also the refurbished theatre with its auditorium newly painted in bronze and black. The stage curtain bore the company's logo, a figure flinging open a gate, while a quartet sung from the musicians' gallery. Using the facilities caused its own wonder as the doors were labelled in a dozen different languages. Those first customers might have wondered if they were still in provincial Dublin. That February night was a cold one and made colder still when the heating system failed to work. The play went down well, although at least one reviewer, CP Curran in the *Irish Statesman*, questioned both the price of the coffee – sixpence a cup – and the programme selling for three pence. One of his readers wrote to the paper to complain about the seats being too hard, too narrow and angled incorrectly to the floor, suggesting that whoever made them should be forced to sit on them for three hours. In his biography *The Boys*, Christopher Fitz-Simon notes the lack of complaints about the prices of the seats, which ranged from 1/3*d* to 4/6*d*.

The first night over, the battle was begun to keep the doors open and it would seem that many played a part. Local universities provided unpaid fodder for minor roles, with students arriving from the likes of the Dublin University Dramatic Society, Trinity College's Elizabethan Society and the Dublin University Players. Wanting to present as international a selection as possible, the theatre staged twenty productions chosen by Hilton Edwards over the following twelve months causing another reviewer, this time the *Irish Independent*'s, to query if this might be too much for the company. This reviewer also found fault with the plays on offer, upsetting Edwards in particular. When he discovered that the critic was the writer Mary Manning (1905–99), he invited her to the theatre where, on meeting her, he told her that he would like to whip her. It was the start of a beautiful friendship, with Edwards going on to produce the play that Manning was writing with her friend Samuel Beckett (1906–89).

By 1930, The Gate was struggling as its founding members relied solely on ticket sales to pay the likes of electrical bills and advertising. They worked as hard as they could, taking part in daily rehearsals and nightly performances and then going home to learn lines for the next play. Edwards directed while MacLiammóir designed the sets and the costumes and they did not stint on ambition. That same year, they closed the theatre for two precious weeks to fully concentrate on staging George Bernard Shaw's *Back to Methuselah*.

The first Annual General Meeting must have been fraught, with the £1,200 shares that remained unsold and the £700 worth of unpaid bills reason enough for it to be proposed to shut the theatre. Naturally, Hilton and MacLiammóir were appalled and would perhaps have been out-voted, had it reached that critical stage. Instead, one of the one-pound shareholders, the wealthy 6th Earl of Longford, Lord Edward Pakenham (1902–61) – a frequent visitor to the theatre with his wife, playwright Lady Christine (1900–80) – offered to buy the £1,200 shares. However, as pointed out by Christopher Fitz-Simon, he did not offer to provide the £700 in arrears. In any case, by buying up the shares he ensured that he was now the major shareholder in the company. There began a happy working relationship between the Longfords and The Gate's founding members that lasted all of five years before being rent asunder in 1936, resulting in the company dividing in two, agreeing to alternate between six months in The Gate and then touring for six months.

The year 1931 was a standout in The Gate's history thanks to an ambitious sixteen-year-old American, newly arrived in Dublin, attending that night's performance of *The Melians: A Tragedy of Imperialism*. He hated the play yet went backstage ostensibly to see a friend but, really, to bump into Edwards and MacLiammóir. The couple were instantly taken by the cigar-smoking youth who introduced himself as Orson Welles (1915–85), a fellow actor offering them his services. They found themselves distracted by his self-confidence, which MacLiammóir later described as 'unquenchable' and granted him an audition for their next production. However, a nervous Welles over-acted, making Edwards laugh, while his partner, although noting that the teenager's performance was as wrong as it could be, also sensed a wondrous potential. Welles was told to spend that night practising sincerity and restraint and to return the following morning, whereby he landed his first professional role. On 13 October 1931, Welles received a rapturous standing ovation for his debut starring role in *Jew Süss* which ultimately proved problematic, sparking jealousy in the heart of MacLíammóir who also struggled at the sight of the American and Edwards embracing in

Orson Welles failed his first audition for The Gate Theatre.

The Gate Theatre.

friendship. Welles appeared in a number of Gate and Peacock productions but started to chaff at the succession of minor roles, although he did make a fine Hamlet, after which he yearned to be Othello. Finally, in February 1932, the ever-ambitious Welles decided to move on to a London stage.

Another big name launched by The Gate was twenty-five-year-old James Mason (1909–84), who was hired after an interview in London. He proved a hit with critics and audiences and thus ran into a similar situation to Orson Welles, having to field the barbs of a jealous MacLiammóir. Mason later confided to a friend that he had considered giving up acting because MacLiammóir had him doubting his talent. Mason's last appearance for The Gate was in *Wuthering Heights* in February 1935.

Other big Irish names that found their footing, career-wise, in The Gate were Geraldine Fitzgerald (1913–2005), Cyril Cusack (1910–93) and Michael Gambon (1940–).

In 1991, The Gate became the first theatre in the world to stage Samuel

Beckett's entire repertoire of nineteen plays.

Over ninety years later, the theatre is still drawing in the crowds thanks to its varied programme, continuing to fulfil Hilton Edwards initial vision of a theatre that would grace its loyal audience with plays from all over the world.

THE ROTUNDA

The oldest maternity hospital in the world was once but a dream for the compassionate and dynamic Doctor Bartholomew Mosse (1712–59). He was determined to improve conditions for nursing mothers after presiding over births in damp cellars and dingy attics. His clergyman father had served as royal chaplain to King William of Orange who rewarded him with the rectorship of Maryborough (Portlaoise), where Mosse was born.

The Rotunda Hospital (pictured here, c. 1776, in reconstructed drawing by Stephen Conlin) was once but a dream for Doctor Bartholomew Mosse.

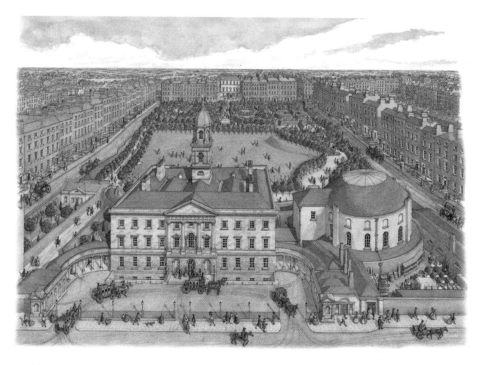

He married Elizabeth Mann in 1737 and, three years later, they welcomed baby Michael into the world. However, both mother and son died soon after which perhaps propelled the doctor to take up an appointment as an army surgeon in Menorca and, then, travel through Europe where he specialised in midwifery, having observed maternity care in several major cities, including Paris. By 1742, he was back in Ireland and married to his cousin Jane Whittingham, with whom he had two children. The following year, he embarked upon a mission to build a maternity hospital in Dublin for the poor.

His first attempt involved taking over a disused theatre in George's Lane, and kitting it out as best he could. It opened on 15 March 1745, the first of its kind in Britain and Ireland, with the first baby 'arriving' five days later.

Doctor Bartholomew Mosse was determined to improve conditions for expectant mothers.

Quite quickly, however, Mosse realised that bigger premises were required and sought to build a hospital from scratch. Furthermore, he wanted it to be beautiful.

To elicit financial aid from his wealthy neighbours and peers in the Dublin Society, of which he was a member, Doctor Mosse embarked upon a demanding campaign, organising concerts, lotteries and balls. When the first performance of George Frideric Handel's (1685–1759) *Messiah* was staged in Dublin, the takings were divided between the Charitable Infirmary and the Mercer's Hospital. Doctor Mosse moved to copy suit, putting on a morality play, *The Distressed Mother*, in the Smock Alley Theatre – but not just for revenue. He wished to normalise a distasteful subject, child-birth, legitimate or otherwise, appealing to the hearts and minds of potential sponsors for his vast project. He took a gamble and won as £150 in tickets were sold along with several yearly subscriptions, at £15, resulting in ten new beds being made available.

Bartholomew Mosse was ahead of his time when babies were usually delivered by untrained midwives and, if a problem arose, then an equally untrained surgeon might be prevailed upon to help. Not every surgeon had the means of studying midwifery in Paris, while both midwife and surgeon knew better than to call on doctors and consultants who despised such messy, noisy work.

As soon as he was able, Doctor Mosse leased four rectangle-shaped acres of flooded waste ground on Great Britain Street (Parnell Street) and hired Robert Stevenson to make him a spectacular garden that he opened to the paying public in 1748. Mosse's New Pleasure Gardens were designed to wow and thus fund the building of the hospital, particularly the following year when lights were added.

The foundation stone was laid in the gardens on 4 June 1751, at nine o'clock in the morning, before a crowd that included Dublin's lord mayor, Thomas Taylor (1707–63). Doctor Mosse, the man of the hour, was treating everyone to a free breakfast and concert, thereby giving the impression of enjoying financial abundance when, in reality, he whispered to a friend that he had but £500 and needed a further £20,000 to build his hospital. His architect of choice was Richard Cassels or Richard Castle in some accounts (1690–1751), Ireland's leading architect, who favoured the Palladian style and had just completed Leinster House on the south side of the River Liffey, which inspired Mosse's vision. The two men apparently enjoyed each other's company, passing many a long night together in a tavern on Fishamble Street. Perhaps it was during these drinking sprees that Mosse dreamt up such decorative features as a tower like the Royal Hospital Kilmainham and Trinity College. In fact, he had wanted the tower to be adorned with a chiming clock with bells, but the locals soon put an end to that particular dream. He wondered about the tower's fundraising potential, briefly considering installing a telescope and observatory, for which he would charge an entrance fee.

Cassels completed the design just before his death in 1751, and the construction was overseen by fellow architect John Ensor (1715–87). In her book *Buildings of Ireland*, Christine Casey describes the hospital as the most influential of Cassel's work in Dublin.

The hospital was opened on 8 December 1757, its grand palatial style paying homage to the beautiful gardens and surrounding area, which by this stage was thoroughly upmarket in tone and inhabitants.

It also included a chapel which proved an important fundraiser, hosting plenty of charity sermons. Christine Casey refers to the chapel's interior as being the most remarkable of its kind in Ireland. Back in 1755, Doctor Mosse had employed Belgian Bartholomew Cramillion (*fl.* 1755–72) to carry out the stucco-work in the chapel for 300 guineas. He was obviously impressed with Cramillion's work as he subsequently offered him 200 guineas in 1757 to work on the altar. The Belgian was worth every penny as what he produced was masterly – life-size figures in relief of Charity,

Faith, Hope and a host of angels and children. Cramillion had yet to be paid for his work when Mosse died in 1759, and was obliged to petition the hospital board in 1760.

When the English poet John Betjeman (1906–84) lived in Ireland as a diplomat during the Second World War, his wife Penelope (1910–86) chose to have their second child in the Rotunda. Their friend, Elizabeth Pakenham (later Lady Longford) (1906–2002) told her that being born in the Rotunda was 'like being born in the Parthenon.'

Following advice, Mosse secured a Royal Charter that transformed his hospital into a national institution and, therefore, was deserving of government aid and a Board of Governors.

All those years of intense work and battling the odds was exhausting and Mosse's health went into decline towards the end of 1758. He made out his will and died virtually penniless the following February at the age of forty-seven. Details about his final months are vague. For example, his death was only briefly mentioned in the minutes of his hospital's board meeting. Also, he was buried in an unmarked grave in Donnybrook Cemetery until the board erected a large head stone that gradually disappeared from sight and eluded searches conducted by Oscar Wilde's father, Sir William (1815–76), amongst others, before its eventual discovery in 1988 when the cemetery was taken over by Dublin Corporation.

At least, Sir Fielding Ould (1710–89), who succeeded Mosse as Master of the hospital, fulfilled Mosse's wish for a large auditorium to be constructed beside the hospital. This building, designed by John Ensor (1715–87) and called The Rotunda, would provide a location for hospital fundraisers such as recitals, concerts and balls.

Doctor Bartholomew Mosse died far too soon but what a legacy he left to Dublin. His gardens stood until the 1940s when they were partially sacrificed to the hospital which was obliged to extend in order to meet the growing demand for its services. A new role for the garden was decreed,

The Garden of Remembrance was formerly part of Doctor Bartholomew Mosse's pleasure gardens.

and architects were invited to submit ideas for a Garden of Remembrance, a memorial to those who had died for Ireland's freedom. In 1946, Daíthí Hanley's (1917–2003) £15,000 idea was chosen as the winner, but then a lengthy debate ensued when an alternative construction – a national concert hall – was suggested for the same spot. The garden was finally built in the 1960s, opening on the fiftieth anniversary of the Easter Rising, although twenty years of indecision proved a costly consequence as its new price was £140,000. Hanley wanted an iconic piece of sculpture to provide a visual snapshot of Irish history, something that referenced the four provinces, which would also be complemented by busts of Irish heroes. In the end, Oisín Kelly's wonderful statue was left to stand alone, the busts forgotten.

ABBEY (FINDLATER'S) CHURCH

Perhaps this church in Parnell Square is not as old as you think. In the 1860s, a prosperous and ever-increasing Protestant population in Dublin required bigger premises in which to gather. Wealthy merchant Alexander

The church was built by wealthy merchant Alexander Findlater for his fellow Protestants.

Findlater (1797–1873) had the means to provide his fellow parishioners with a new and improved place of worship, and bought land in Rutland Square (now Parnell Square), paying £14,000 to have a church (Abbey Church) designed and built. His reward was surely a place in Heaven as well as the church being informally named after him forevermore.

Born in Glasgow, Alexander had experienced poverty after his father died suddenly, leaving his large family in dire straits and obliging his wife to take in lodgers. As soon as he was old enough, he followed his older brother William into the shipping industry, working as a shipbroker in Greenock, close to Glasgow. At sixteen he took a job in Newfoundland, working for a company that traded in dried cod, doing their accounts and overseeing the catching and drying out of the fish. It was invaluable experience that would stand to him in his later career. When the company folded, Alexander moved on to Quebec and then Montreal before returning to

Scotland. In 1823, at the age of twenty-six, he moved to Dublin – possibly in response to his friends William and Gilbert Burns, nephews of the famous poet Robert (1759–96), who had gone to Dublin to set themselves up in business. Meanwhile, William Findlater had married a Donegal woman, Sophia Huntington of Fahan, and moved to Derry where he worked as a shipbroker.

His uncle, a customs officer in Glasgow, provided Alexander with a letter of introduction for a colleague in Dublin's Custom House. He was soon dealing in whiskey, taking advantage of the recent fifty-six per cent drop in duties on spirits to help legal distilleries properly compete with the illegal traders. The next seven years were busy and immensely productive. Starting out in 1828 on Burgh Quay in premises opposite the Custom House, as The Irish & Scotch Whiskey Stores, Alexander relied on a network of friends and family to fulfil every aspect of his business. By 1830 he had several branches in Dublin and Kingstown (Dún Laoghaire) and was able to bring his mother to live in Dublin. He was also selling a lot more than

whiskey, importing the likes of English meat, Dunlop cheese, wine, sherry, port, rum, soap, coffee, dried fruit and tobacco.

Several premises and several years later, in 1835, he leased a large property on 27-32 Upper Sackville Street and began trading as Findlater, Lennox & Co.

He was still a bachelor but a family man at heart. For instance, when his brother William died in 1831, he paid for his seven-year-old nephew's schooling

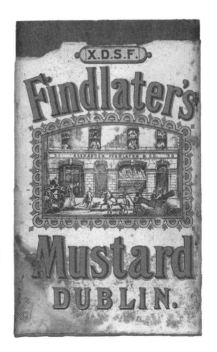

Findlater's Mustard label.

and contributed towards the education of William's three daughters. He also paid his mother a regular allowance. A second tragedy befell the family in 1836 with the death of a second brother, John, a sea captain whose ship the *James Laurie* went down off the coast of the Bahamas with the loss of all on board. John's wife Mary Anne died the following year from TB, thus making orphans of their four children. Alexander took on complete financial responsibility for the children, who went to live with his sister Susanna and her husband Captain John Snowden. His other sister, Helen, was widowed in 1841 and Alexander paid for her children's education and upkeep.

It is hardly surprising that Alexander provided a church. Architect Andrew Heiton (1823–94) created a Gothic build that fairly graced the area with its elegant towers, including a 150–foot (45.72-metre) spire and French-styled decoration.

Gothic architecture originated in France when the historian and advisor to kings Abbot Suger (*c.* 1081–1151) had the chancel of his church, the Abbey of Saint-Denis, redesigned in the late 1130s, with an eye towards including as much light and space as possible. His inspiration was the triumphal arch to the Emperor Constantine (*c.* 272–337) in Rome and its three-portal structure. Abbot Suger's church would become the first Gothic building. The style quickly caught on, especially in relation to church builds of all sizes. Gothic architecture exaggerated features like the number and size of stained-glass windows and decorative arches, whilst the actual churches themselves, using flying buttresses to support their walls, were built wondrously tall, as if to stretch all the way to Heaven itself.

The foundation stone for the Abbey Church was laid in November 1862 and opened for business a couple of years later in October, at an approximate cost of £13,000. Its first pastor was John Hall (1829–98) who, in 1867, would take up the invitation to be pastor at the Fifth Avenue Presbyterian Church in New York. Built by Samuel Henry Bolton (1828–97), Abbey Church was given an impressive write up in *Saunder's Newsletter*, describing how it was built with Dalkey granite that had been treated with Portland stone. A grateful congregation paid for a memorial window that depicted Findlater's family arms with the words: *To commemorate the munificence, and to perpetuate the name of Alexander Findlater, the founder and donor of this church.*

Inside, the centre was illuminated by six medieval coronas (chandeliers), holding thirty lights each, while lanterns were hung throughout on the stairs and in the vestibules. The plush red seats could hold 850 people who would be comfortable in winter thanks to indoor heating. The building also included an underground classroom with further rooms upstairs, behind the church. James Ballantyne (1806–77), the Scottish artist and writer, supplied the beautiful stained-glass windows from his Edinburgh studio.

It seems that Alexander Findlater's entire life centred around the making and then the gifting of money to deserving folk and projects. He continued to establish new businesses with new partners, including setting up his own brewery after watching the Guinness brewery flourish thanks to a new preference for beer. He funded more church builds, including giving £1,000 to St Andrew's Church of Ireland in Suffolk Street in 1869. And other faiths benefitted too. For instance, he gave money to a Catholic church in Monkstown, a Presbyterian church in Rathgar and also to a Methodist chapel. Aside from churches, he helped finance such hospitals as Donnybrook's Royal Hospital for Incurables. In fact, it is believed that he made annual payments to 150 charities while he lived.

Financing a church build was not a unique project for a man of his calling. St Patrick's Cathedral was refurbished thanks to the deep pockets of Benjamin Lee Guinness, while the prosperous whiskey merchant Henry Roe almost bankrupted himself in paying for the reconstruction of Christ Church Cathedral in 1870.

In 1860, after he had finished paying for the education of various nephews and nieces, Alexander spent £2,000 on a house in Monkstown, big enough for himself and his two widowed sisters, Helen and Susanna. Susanna ran the household and for this received a weekly wage from her brother. Her death in 1871 hit him hard and he died two years later on 8 August at the age of seventy-six. His funeral confirmed his popularity and was well attended by rich and poor alike. The coffin was placed into a carriage that left the Monkstown house at 9.15am. By the time it reached the South Circular Road on its way to Mount Jerome Cemetery, it was being tailed by over two hundred carriages of mourners and plenty more were on foot. His obituary in *The Irish Times* lauded him for his generosity to charities of all creed and paid him a high compliment of acknowledging his Scottish origins before stating that, 'once he settled amongst us, he became as Irish as the Irish themselves'.

CLERYS DEPARTMENT STORE

In 1852, five neighbouring premises on Sackville Street, previously home to five drapery stores, were demolished in order to free up one large site for something far classier on a grand scale. In May the following year, McSwiney, Delany & Co opened their massive department store, the Palatial Mart, providing upmarket shoppers with something new.

Future Lord Mayor of Dublin twice-over Peter Paul McSwiney (1809/10–1884) was a first cousin of James Joyce's father, John Stanislaus, and a big fan of Daniel O'Connell. In fact, on 8 August 1862, it was McSwiney who laid the foundation stone in Glasnevin Cemetery for the O'Connell Memorial Round Tower.

George Delany's (*d.* 1906) retirement in 1872 left his partner as chairman of Dublin's first public company.

For nineteenth-century Dubliners, the Palatial was a unique shopping experience. As a new build, five storeys high, with huge windows overlooking Sackville Street, the Palatial can be called the world's first purpose-built department store. Inside must have seemed spectacular; one stepped into what appeared to be a great hall punctuated by stately Corinthian pillars directing one's attention upwards to the galleries that could be accessed by ornate staircases.

Inevitably, it proved unpopular with small shopkeepers who referred to it as 'a monster store'.

The Palatial targeted the best of customers– those with deep pockets and nice accents, who required their parcels to be delivered to their homes and settled their accounts on a monthly basis.

Staff lived in and slept in dormitories upstairs, until the early twentieth century. Up beyond the galleries, they had their own dining hall and even library. The 1901 census shows 105 staff living on the premises.

In her article for *History Ireland*, Stephanie Rains writes about how the Palatial, which sold everything from wellington boots to houseware, initially dominated the shopping scene in Sackville Street. Following a lengthy boom, McSwiney spent £50,000 extending the store in 1878, incorporating part of the Imperial Hotel – which remained a separate business – adding three bays to the front of the building, making a total of eleven. Furthermore, McSwiney had the original windows replaced with the recently developed large plate-glass windows.

He may have regretted this move when, the following year, Ireland was hit with a depression and the massive store found itself in straitened circumstances. McSwiney was obliged to take on partners and, eventually, illness forced him to retire. In 1882, the store went bankrupt and was hastily renamed the Dublin Drapery Warehouse. However, business continued to spiral and the shop was put into liquidation. A group of buyers and principal investors stepped forward, including Tipperary man Michael John Clery (1834–96), William Martin Murphy (1845–1919) and Murphy's father-in-law, James Fitzgerald Lombard (1817–1901), who topped the board for Arnott's department store. Michael John Clery bought the mart

William Martin Murphy was one of the initial investors for the new store Clery & Company.

for a song, at £32,000; it had been recently valued at £40,000. The store underwent a third name change, this time to Clery & Company, and opened in time for Christmas shopping in 1884.

Like McSwiney before him, Michael John Clery was politically active. Following the arrest of *The Nation*'s editor, Charles Gavan Duffy (1816–1903), Clery briefly edited the paper. When he died in 1898, Clery, the former draper's assistant, was a millionaire. That same year his store was incorporated as 'Clery & Company Ltd – General drapers, house furnishers and booksellers'.

Chaotic times ensued for both the store and the country. Robert Clery took over his father's store only to die in 1900. When his heir died of flu in France in 1918, the store was passed to his son-in-law (Sir) Christopher Nixon.

The store struck a sour note with booksellers in the late 1890s when they began selling cheap books. At a booksellers' meeting across the street in Eason, it was proposed to contact English publishers who were supplying the likes of drapers' stores with books that were being heavily discounted. One publisher, Longman's, proved obstinate, refusing to break off its relationship with Clery's. In 1904, Clery's signed the newly created Net Book Agreement, though Dublin booksellers resented the store being recognised as a peer trader by the Publishers' Association which had been founded in 1896.

The building saw quite a bit of action that fateful week of the Rising in 1916. On Easter Monday, 24 April, Pádraig Pearse, Seán Macdiarmada and James Connolly were bitterly disappointed in Dublin's poor as they watched men, women and children enter into the spirit of revolution with some old-fashioned looting. Clery's was hard hit, the windows smashed and the doors broken open. Connolly tasked future president of Ireland, Seán Thomas O'Kelly (1882–1966), with disbanding the looters. Accompanied by twelve armed men, O'Kelly marched into a besieged Clery's. When his call for order was ignored, he and his men resorted to using their batons and firing bullets into the ceiling, chasing offenders out of the shop.

Future president of Ireland Seán Thomas O'Kelly (pictured here on the left, with Denis Guiney standing in background) could not bring himself to shoot looters.

Eventually, they managed to clear the place and moved onto the next store. Within minutes, Clery's was overrun again.

O'Kelly returned to the GPO to inform Connolly that his task was an impossible one. Connolly told him he should have shot some of the looters, leaving O'Kelly feeling that he had failed Ireland in some way.

A few days later, the building that housed Clery's and the Imperial Hotel burnt to the ground. Oscar Traynor (1886–1963), Ireland's future Minister for Justice, who, in 1916, was in command of the Metropole garrison, swore he saw the plate-glass windows melt away in the fire. Two months later, Clery's was back in business in a new, temporary location – the Metropolitan Hall in Lower Abbey Street. Six years would pass before the store returned to its rightful place, reopening on O'Connell Street in August 1922. The new build cost £400,000, although half of this was paid by the government's compensation scheme for damage caused by the Rising.

The architect was Englishman Robert Francis Atkinson (1869–1923), who had been involved in designing Selfridges in Oxford Street, London, which was the inspiration for this new Clery's.

In the book *Dublin, 1910–1940: Shaping the City & Suburbs*, Ruth McManus discusses 1920's O'Connell Street and its reliance on Clery's Department Store for creating footfall. Henry Street had superior pulling power thanks to its wide range of shops, but Clery's did its best for O'Connell Street, describing the thoroughfare, in its own promotional material, as the 'finest and busiest street in Ireland'.

Within a year of reopening its doors, Clery's was already struggling. Chairman William Murphy decided that a new managing director was called for and chose the experienced John McGuire, while John's son, Edward, was made assistant manager. Some felt that Murphy was looking for a scapegoat should the business go under.

Taking the helm of the famous store that was running at a loss was going to be a challenge but one that John McGuire felt he was up to, provided he

John McGuire, who created huge profits for Clery's department store.

was left alone to do it. To that end, McGuire's contract stipulated that he have complete and sole control of the company for the next fifteen years. He also wanted £5,000 a year along with half the profits over £9,000. The board wisely agreed to all his requests as, twelve months later, Clery's profits exceeded £10,000. That figure soared over the next ten years, reaching an annual average of £475,000, while netting McGuire almost £50,000 in commission.

All was very well indeed aside from one little nugget of discontent: the shareholders, most of whom were on the board of directors, had received no dividends.

Meanwhile, the new Clery's was much bigger and worked hard at attracting not just Dubliners but rural customers, establishing itself as what Joseph Brady calls a national store. In *Dublin, 1930–1950: The Emergence of the Modern City*, Brady describes how Clery's put out a pamphlet in the mid-1930s, boasting 15,000 customers daily, with that figure tripling during the Christmas boom. The board hit upon the beauty that was the

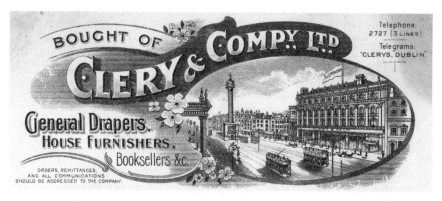

Late nineteenth-century billhead for Clery's department store, showing the extent of the premises and electric trams on Sackville Street.

rail excursion, whereby they targeted those living outside Dublin, providing them with a special rate train fare to come and do their shopping in the capital city. Customers availing of these deals, understood that, although they were not actually obliged to shop in Clery's, spending over £5 in the store resulted in Clery's refunding their train ticket.

At this stage, there were fifty-three departments spread over four storeys, along with a bargain basement where old stock was sold at knock-down prices. Presumably it is the basement that James Joyce references in 'Nausicaa', chapter thirteen of *Ulysses*, when the tastefully dressed Gerty MacDowell sets out in search of the right material to match the egg-blue chenille of her straw hat. We don't know where she begins her search but we are told that it takes up all Tuesday afternoon until she lands at Clery's and finds exactly what she wants, albeit 'slightly shop soiled', but at the perfect price.

To attract customers downstairs, a soda fountain was set up to provide ice-cream and sugary drinks. The basement was also home to the grocery store. One of the busiest departments was devoted to the needs of the modern woman, selling everything from material and needlework to clothes, jewellery and handbags. A more refined version of this department, the 'Ladies' Domain', was upstairs in the Grand Gallery, where one could buy underwear and party wear. Further temptation was provided by the in-house hairdresser and beauty salon. In their advertisements, Clery's swore to sell only the most up-to-date clothes made from the best material. The Menswear department wasn't immediately apparent; it was slightly hidden to the side, selling clothes, hats and sportswear.

The ground floor was dominated by the household department, selling blankets, curtains, rugs and so on, while the big item ticket – furniture – required more space on the top floor. Clery's provided for minor medical needs, with its own pharmacy and optician. It also catered for those with a sweet-tooth and/or a liking for tobacco. On top of all that, there was even a department that sold vestments and accessories for priests.

Of course, there was a restaurant too, with full table service. And it was big, with a maximum capacity of 500 diners. During the mid–1930s, it opened six days a week from 9am to 8pm, staying open after the store closed on Saturdays at 1pm. Lunch was served between 12.30 and 3.30pm and, surprisingly, the prices were reasonable. For instance, high tea could be got for a shilling and six pence. If the restaurant was too busy, you could relax in the 'coffee lounge'.

Maintaining local customers required wheels and lots of them. Clery's vans delivered parcels up to twenty miles from the city centre, while anyone living beyond that had their goods posted to them. Long before online shopping, Clery's were dealing with approximately 700 orders on a daily basis. A lot of money was spent in keeping customers up to date, by post, with new stock. Furthermore, six sales representatives provided a one-on-one personal shopper experience for customers across England and Ireland who could not travel to the store.

Having secured Clery's as the number one store for Irish consumers, the next challenge was attracting the international customers who sailed into Dublin on the cruise ships.

The January 1933 accounts showed a whopping £553,441 in sales, with a net profit of £15,460, while elsewhere, Wall Street's 1929 stock market crash was making itself felt. Clery's board of directors decided they no longer needed McGuire's services and, six years short of his contracted reign, made their move. William Lombard, who had put £80,000 of his own money into Clery's in 1922, understandably wanted it back, but John McGuire refused to do so until he was paid his commission. Relations soured, and McGuire was dismissed for what was described as 'misconduct', that is, his refusal to pay out the dividends to the shareholders. He sued the board for wrongful dismissal.

It went to court, where Judge Hanna ruled that the board had no right to devise such a contract with McGuire in the first place. In other words, the board won. McGuire's son, Edward, felt that Murphy knew full well that the contract was flimsy but had not expected McGuire to prove so effective in transforming Clery's fortune.

Towards the end of the 1930s the business was struggling. Clery's imported a lot of their goods from abroad and this reliance on foreign products was quickly made precarious due to the outbreak of war. By this stage, Sir Christopher Nixon was now Managing Director and could do little to stem the loss in sales and revenue.

In 1936, the Equity and Law Life Assurance Company loaned Clery's £200,000. Four years later, Sir Christopher put in £20,000 of his own money and tried to find a buyer for the store, with the creditors nipping at his heels. The board discussed liquidation, while the anxious staff offered to take a pay cut. However, the end was surely inevitable with that outstanding £200,000 for Equity and Law Life Assurance, Clery's biggest creditor, and the directors put the store into receivership in 1940. The receiver, Eustace Shott of Craig Gardner & Co, closed the store, got rid of the staff and set about selling the company's assets in wartime, no mean feat.

In November, Shott approached Clery's profitable neighbour Denis Guiney (1893–1967), who ran his successful shop around the corner in

Talbot Street. Interested, Guiney had Shott walk him through Clery's for a brief look at its stock and fittings. Two days later, he made an initial offer of £225,000, warning Shott that he wanted a quick answer in order to cash in on the Christmas season. Following a creditors' meeting, this offer was raised to £250,000 with most of it going to staff that had previously invested their life savings in the company in order to help save it.

Guiney paid the £20,000 deposit and promptly took over the store, the balance being raised from the Munster and Leinster Bank. Not everyone was happy with the outcome. Sir Christopher and his peers felt Guiney had paid too cheap a price and took him and Shott to court to have the sale annulled. The judge disagreed, however, leaving Denis Guiney free to work his magic on his new store. He reopened Clery's on Friday, 29 November 1940, with a massive sale, in which all stock was being sold at bargain prices. The customers turned up in their thousands, making Clery's £45,000 that very first week. Guiney subscribed to the ethos of small profits and quick turnover.

He set about investing big money into smartening up the restaurant and spending £82,000 on a huge ballroom that could hold up to 500 guests along with a full orchestra. In 1943, following several attempts, he got a bar licence. In all, he spent £250,000 and it proved to be a wise investment. When the ballroom, restaurants and the Beehive bar opened in 1944, they were an instant hit. Clery's was the place to be throughout the 1950s and 1960s. In 1956, Fianna Fáil politician and future Taoiseach Seán Lemass gave his historical speech in the ballroom, launching his new economic vision for Ireland that signalled a break from the de Valera era.

Meanwhile, the store flourished thanks to its new owner, and by 1960, it was the biggest and most successful shop in Ireland, establishing Guiney as a household name. A popular employer for forty-six years, he was responsible for supplying approximately 6,000 Irish people with jobs. One of his employees was sales assistant Mary Leahy (1901–2004) from County Limerick, whom he had married in 1938 following the death of

Denis Guiney and his second wife, former sales assistant Mary Leahy.

his first wife, Nora.

Another employee was Ireland's successful amateur golfer Philomena Garvey (1926–2009), who worked in the sports department. Her victories included the 1957 British Open Amateur Ladies Championship.

To be sure, Guiney courted a plainer, less-monied customer with his bargains and he proved quite sensitive when he saw a customer stuff her newly purchased hat, and its Clery's bag, into another bag that belonged to a more expensive store. Imagine her mortification when he accosted her and said:

> Madame, if you won't be seen carrying my bag, you won't be seen wearing my hat. Take that hat upstairs and the sales lady will refund you your money.

Following his death in 1967, his wife Mary became the chairperson and main shareholder of the company, while their nephew, Arthur Walls (1925–2000), took over the day-to-day running of the store. It was Walls who unveiled the new clock, designed by Christopher Stokes in Cork, at precisely a quarter to eleven, to the crowd that had gathered on a wet morning in October 1990. The clock and event commemorated the fiftieth anniversary of Denis Guiney's buying the company. Caught up in the

Clery's clock was a popular meeting point for generations of Dubliners.

moment, Walls declared for all to hear that 'Clery's goes on and on forever!'

In 2001, an article in the *Irish Independent* described Clery's as a record-breaker because it was the only department store worldwide that was owned by a centenarian, who was, of course, Mary Guiney.

When Mrs Guiney died, at the age of a hundred and three, Liam Reid, writing in *The Irish Times* described her as 'a formidable woman ... who remained the power behind the empire ....' She had had plenty to contend with, seeing off several attempts to buy out the Guiney family and turn the store into a hotel. In 1999, she rejected at least two takeover bids worth 30 million pounds. Her argument was plain: 'Why would I want to sell the best business and building in Ireland?'

A long-time fan of O'Connell Street, Chairwoman Guiney supported recent changes like the Spire and the Luas tracks, believing that they would regenerate the street and the surrounding area.

Meanwhile, in response to customers migrating to the new shopping centres opening up in the suburbs, Clery's opened up small outlets in the likes of Blanchardstown and the Square Shopping Centre in Tallaght.

Reid finished his article by describing Clery's as 'one of the most valuable retail buildings in the country.' However, he also writes that the store made less than €72,000 in the year ending January 2004, surmising that this poor show might attract further attempts to buy out the company.

Eight years later and the store went into receivership again. On 18 September 2012, the *Irish Independent* broke the news that the store had been sold to an American private equity firm the previous evening, whose chief executive pledged to keep on the 147 members of staff. What followed was nothing short of a tragedy. Less than three years later, Clery's was sold for one euro in the early hours of Friday, 12 January 2015 and, by Friday night, was gone. The building was sold for 29 million euro to the Natrium Investment Group. That Friday, at 6pm, 130 staff along with 330 concession owners were told the store was no more. Some of the staff had worked there for decades. Furthermore, they were told that there was no money for redundancies. In other words, the State was obliged to pay the 2.5 million-euro redundancy bill. A bitter fight ensued between staff and the new owners, which was only resolved in March 2017 when SIPTU announced that Natrium had finally made a goodwill payment to all staff.

Having bought the building for 29 million euro, Natrium sold it on in October 2018 for 63 million. Construction work began the following year, with the old building being transformed in order to house a hotel, retail and office space, bars and restaurants. It is hoped that the new projects will inject new energy and businesses into the area, thereby doing what Clery's has done before – help save O'Connell Street.

EASON

In his *Eason & Son: A History*, LM Cullen introduces us to Somerset-born Charles Eason Snr (*d.* 1899), who arrived in Dublin in 1856 to manage the new Irish extension of the newsagent wholesaler on Sackville Street for William

View of Tyler's, Eason's, and the Metropole on O'Connell Street, 1972.

Henry Smith (1792–1865). He had started working for the company six years earlier, taking over their bookstall at Victoria Station in Manchester.

Eason was a worrier who never allowed himself to relax. Most of his anxiety stemmed from the job but he also spent time worrying about his health. According to letters he wrote to his mother, he fell victim to bad colds every winter – Irish weather did not agree with him – and he was also a martyr to gout. Cullen suggests that he might have been a hypochondriac or, at least, had hypochondriacal tendencies. When Smith visited his employee and business in December 1858, he wrote to his wife praising Eason's honesty and goodness but also described him as '… an odd little fellow, and you would laugh at him ….'

The business grew quickly. In 1856, Charles Eason was the sole supervisor of the entire operation. Smith sent him a letter advising against erecting a high partition to separate his office from the goings-on on the floor as it was better that he should be able to see everything from his desk. At this time, the staff numbered less than forty. Twenty years later, however, there were 136 employees and, a decade after that, in 1886, this number had grown to 175.

According to the wage books, 1862 was the year of change, heralding in a proper structure that evolved around a shop, a wholesale division and a book department. Two men worked in the stables, with papers and mail being delivered by horse and carriage, whilst a third worked in the railway advertising workshop. All changed again in 1869 with the splitting of the wholesale department into two factions: one focusing on city business and the second focusing on the country at large. As a consequence, administration had to upgrade its affairs and a proper accountancy was established with a counting house. Meanwhile, the two men in the stables were now five and the railway advertising got its own department. A printing office was opened, along with a 'stock' department, which, over time, would morph into the stationery department.

Finally, in 1875, the company we recognise today was established with the further divvying up of roles. The wholesale department was sectioned off into news, books and stationery. Two offices now housed accounts and the cashiers separately, but the biggest change was the printing department that had been set up to provide the staff with their own stationery and order sheets for their trade customers. Employing just five in 1869, the increase in staff was a steady one until there were twenty at work in that single department in 1901.

The prayer-book department was also thriving, obliging Charles Eason to give it its own storeroom on Aston Quay.

In 1865, a Mr Dewar, who was Scottish, was hired to oversee the wholesale department and for this was paid more than anyone else. Ten years later, James Dignam was made head of Wholesale News and he and Dewar clashed frequently. James Dignam wrote travel guides to places he had never visited. His Spanish guide included the marvellous line, 'The river Garonne is the driest river in Europe.' He also boasted of meeting the pope in Rome. According to Dignam, when the Holy See heard his name, he responded, 'Is that you, James?'

Henry Digges joined the firm in 1866 and was still there fifty-nine years later in 1925, making a presentation to Charles Eason Jnr (*b.* 1843), to mark his fifty years in Eason's. Charles took over the firm after his father's death in 1889. In 1936, Henry Digges attended the anniversary celebrations of Eason & Son's as an independent business.

Perhaps one of Charles Eason's (Snr) most important initiatives was his creation of a stationery section in response to the population's new-found interest in writing letters. For instance, the years between 1843 and 1857 saw a gigantic leap in sending letters, from 23.4 to 42 million, an obvious indication that there had been a massive growth in literacy.

Playwright Seán O'Casey was fired about a week after he started working in Eason's. In his 1942 memoir, *Pictures in the Hallway*, he provides a description of a typical frantic morning spent receiving the newspapers and getting them sorted for the bookstalls around the country. Initially, the day began at 6am for the wholesale news department but, over the next few years, as the demand for papers grew, the office began opening at 5am in 1872. This was a job for strong men and boys and plenty were let go when they proved unable to carry the heavy loads. O'Casey writes that the morning began with what appeared as organised chaos. A van delivered countless bundles of the *Freeman Journal*, *The Irish Times* and the *Irish Independent* prompting a sort of melée as an army of workers – men and boys – rushed out to grab them as fast as they could, some actually staggering with their load as they hurried to bring them inside and sort them out for their respective destinations.

Once his handcart was full, O'Casey took off to make his deliveries to the Belfast train at Amiens Street Station (now Connolly Station), amongst others. It was only on his return that he could have his break-

fast, for which he received an allowance. One suspects he knew exactly what he was doing when he went to the cashier's office to receive his first wages and refused to remove his cap. The sensitive cashier demanded that Charles Eason Jnr himself deal with such thuggery. When Mr Eason arrived on the scene, he wasted no time in taking sides, bellowing

Seán O'Casey worked for a short time at Eason's on O'Connell Street.

Eason's and the then tree-lined mall of O'Connell Street.

to the cashier to hand over O'Casey's wages: 'Let him have, let him have it, and go!' Eason's parting shot was 'God bless us, how did such a person ever come to be employed!'

It is a funny story but also a good insight into the level of discipline exacted, although it would appear that newer recruits had to meet an even higher standard than their long-term colleagues. For instance, in 1878, Charles Eason Snr noted down: 'Bligh – worse for liquor Tuesday, took pledge on Wednesday.' Drunkenness was surely worse than wearing a cap in the cashier's office. Whoever Bligh was, he was in trouble again in 1887 for drinking and fighting. No sign of his dismissal, merely a reprimand.

Eason's became an unwitting host in April 1916. During the Easter Rising, on Tuesday, 25 April, having been alerted to disturbances in Dublin, Charles Eason Jnr left his Dalkey home to take a train to Bray and then a second one to Harcourt Street. The all-important issue was the distribution of the newspapers. From Harcourt Street, Charles walked to his younger brother Fred's (*d.* 1964) house in Kenilworth Square, meeting staff who had brought copies of *The Irish Times* there. One of the directors, Albert Brunton, was at the office along with over thirty staff. One devoted employee offered to run to *The Irish Times* office and returned with 200 copies. His labour was in vain, however, as not one paper sold.

Brunton sent the staff home, asking two or three men to remain overnight to guard the premises from looters, after watching raucous locals descend on vulnerable, smaller shops on Sackville Street. It was hard to know exactly what was going on. Telephone operators were prioritising military calls pertaining to the rebellion and one learned pretty quickly that questions regarding whether a shop could continue trading in news and stationery were not a priority. Those on guard in Eason's were 'ambushed' during tea hour by a group of rebels who had dug their way through from next door's Metropole Hotel. The staff were told to leave, the intruders promising not to cause any damage unless shots were fired signifying that all would then be out of their control. Well, shots were fired, of course. According to Thomas Coffey's book *Agony at Easter*, it was James Connolly

O'Connell Street after the 1916 Rising, with a barricade and the ruined remains of Freeman Telegraph offices. Eason's was also one of the businesses to incur severe damage.

who decided that a barricade was needed in front of Eason's and one was hastily put together using books and furniture.

The following morning, an employee turned up for work and not only was he barred entrance to the premises, but he was also relieved of his keys. Somehow, he managed to get a call through to Charles Eason at 7.30am to explain the circumstances. The Eason family moved fast. Fred's house in Rathgar became the new hub and staff were instructed to make their way there, via an advertisement printed in Thursday's *Irish Times*.

Charles stayed in Fred's and, on Thursday morning, attempted to get into the city centre. Rumours were spiralling about looting and broken windows. Apparently, shots were being fired from inside Eason's, which necessitated the breaking of glass. Blockades at Portobello Bridge made Charles turn around again and he was slightly shaken at the absence of police. He worried about the growing scarcity of food, predicting riots if care was not taken.

On Friday, 28 April, Charles made another attempt, this time reaching the corner of St Stephen's Green, before changing his mind at the sound of gunfire. He also heard something about buildings being on fire in Sackville Street.

In fact, Friday was to prove a pivotal day, both for the rebels in the burn-ing GPO and for Eason's with the return of normal business. Newspapers arrived from Holyhead, including a backlog of parcels. Eason's bookstall at Kingstown received its quota of newspapers, while papers were also deliv-ered to Bray and Dalkey. Furthermore, a successful application was made for a pass to get newspapers to Kenilworth Square. Meanwhile, hardcore cash had been obtained, allowing the cashier to pay wages to any staff who turned up between 4 and 8pm that evening.

On the following day, Saturday, the word on the streets was that the rebels had surrendered. The Rising was all over.

In Dalkey, on Sunday, 30 April, Charles Eason and his son John Charles

Malcolm (1880–1976) were obliged to get in line in the town hall to obtain permits to enter the city centre. They were lucky. One of the attending officers was a former employee of Eason's and he allowed them go ahead of everyone else. John Charles cycled into town but could not reach Sackville Street as shots were still being fired at the rebels who had spilled out into nearby tenements and houses.

On Sunday, 1 May, they were able to drive into town to find their store destroyed. However, this did not mean the end of Eason's, and just two weeks later, they were back in business in two temporary properties. Once the burnt-out skeleton of their Abbey Street/Sackville Street premises had been pulled down, a wooden hut was erected and customers resumed their newspaper and magazine habits amidst the still-smoking ruins. A new location had to be found when construction workers arrived to begin the rebuild and the wooden shack was exchanged for 50 Sackville Street. One must admire the simple genius of whomever it was in Eason's that came up with the idea to publish a book of photographs, *The Rebellion in Dublin*, which recorded Dublin's devastation in June 1916. It was an instant hit, although the book was condemned for laying the blame of the multiple fires at the feet of the Volunteers, accusing them of firing on the fire brigade. In fairness, the fire brigade did find themselves under attack as they fought infernos all over town. Fire brigade chief Captain Purcell was applauded by onlookers on Sackville Street as he drove his horse and carriage up and down the street, ignoring the bullets. Meanwhile, two newsagents, one in Carrick-on-Suir and one in Clonmel, were told not to sell the Eason's book, while Eason's themselves admitted that it would not be on display in their window.

The company was compensated for their loss. Following inspection, they claimed £32,626 for the building and received a little less, at £27,252. They claimed just over £10,000 for furniture and, again, received a little less, at £9,156. They put in a claim for £20,577 to cover the loss of stock and were rewarded £19,442. All in all, their total reward of £55,850 was £8,000 short of their total claim for £63,329. And they put it to good use.

Scottish locomotive engineer, John Alexander Cameron Ruthven (*b*. 1850/1), who managed the railway advertising department, undoubtedly never expected to have to design an entire new building for work. He created one large premises out of what had been two separate locations between Middle Abbey and Sackville Street. Ruthven's design required steps to access the building as he had raised the level of the first floor, thus allowing for a bigger and deeper basement.

Eason's staff and stock moved into the new wholesale premises in October 1919 and, six months later, the shop was finally opened. The smell of fresh paint, fresh wood and new potential in retail must have been hampered by the smell of unrest in Dublin 1919. Things were afoot and, as always, the initial warning signs were modest. Killing the 1916 rebels lit a flame, a hatred for all things English and that included their newspapers, upon which half of Eason's yield was based.

Charles Eason fretted about being forced to prove his loyalties to those who were actually in charge by taking a stance against Sinn Féin. On 20 April 1921, the Trade Department of Dáil Éireann issued a letter in which they shared their proposal to prevent any shop from selling British Christmas cards. Then, when that proposal did come into effect the following January, they set their eyes on British pictorial calendars. Censorship spread like the flu.

Newspaper distribution depended on the trains, which were hit by a series of strikes, and in 1920, there were no trains for ten days because railway workers refused to handle anything – including trains – that involved the military.

With the introduction of a curfew on 24 February 1920, permits were now required for the vans delivering the papers to stations and bookstalls. Eason pleaded for lenience and must have been relieved to have received a letter from a Dublin Castle employee, identifying himself as a customer and promising to arrange the necessary permits.

Then the staff were subjected to raids such as the two that took place on 8 November 1920 when the premises were surrounded and approximately 160 male employees were taken to the boardroom, one by one, to be grilled on what they had done in 1916 and whether they were a member of any club or had ever been in the Volunteers. John Charles Eason left a description of that nerve-wracking day and how employees strove to keep one another calm. In response to the tension, smoking on the premises was permitted, having been previously disallowed.

Of course, there were employees with links to various organisations, while several had been involved in the Rising, but their jobs were still there for them afterwards. Meanwhile, at least one employee was related to an officer in the RIC, which surely muddied the atmosphere.

In August 1920, the Pembroke Sinn Féin committee banned the selling of English Sunday newspapers, resulting in armed men preventing Eason's delivery vans from travelling out of the city centre. The ensuing hullabaloo from retailers made Arthur Griffith (1871–1922) promise to look into suspending the ban, yet a few months later in October, John Toms, Eason's sales representative, discovered that shops in Tipperary were being instructed to cancel their English newspapers. Then, in December, a notice was sent to various newsagents in Lismore from the 'Customs Dept IRA', explaining their 'determination to wipe out English literature'. They also ordered shops not to accept papers such as *News of the World* and *Daily Sketch* from Eason's. The notice ended with a polite threat: 'Please spare us any further trouble by doing the right thing at once.' One cannot fail to hear the invisible tag-on, 'or else'.

This was just the beginning. The following year brought a quickening in the form of the Dáil issuing a boycott of all products from Belfast. Eason's compromised; they stopped buying Belfast goods *apart* from newspapers.

On 9 December 1921, the Dáil sent a message 'to cease the sale of all Belfast papers'. Charles Eason went to the Mansion House to protest this latest decision and ask for it to be reversed. He was successful for a time. An IRA convention in March discussed the desire to strengthen the boycott once more. Meanwhile, complaints were raised in the Dáil about the Irish newspapers with Éamon de Valera lamenting their seemingly lack of interest in atrocities carried out in the north.

The *Freeman's Journal* responded by criticising de Valera, which resulted in a Tubbercurry newsagent, at least, being ordered not to sell the journal, whilst delivery vans were searched to ensure they did not contain the offending paper. On 13 April 1922, a stack of Belfast papers sitting on the counter in Eason's were seized and the company was fined £100 for ignoring the boycott. One comical aside was when the government's Press Room Department complained to Eason's about not receiving their copies of *The Irish News* and Eason's were obliged to point the finger back in their direction.

Civil war finally broke out on 28 June with Free State soldiers firing on the Four Courts. Few staff turned up for work that day and normal distribution of the papers was impossible due to delayed or cancelled train services. One delivery van was seized after it had been found to contain English newspapers. Two days later, on Friday, 30 June, Eason's closed their doors at 1pm in response to terrific gun battles outside. The following Monday morning Mr EW Hallett, the accountant, opened the premises for the few employees who managed to turn up. However, the Red Cross needed it as there was fighting all around Sackville Street. By 7 July, the situation had calmed and just about the entire 5am shift turned up for work, but interrupted train services played havoc with deliveries. The company also lost several staff who were summoned for Free State Service. Meanwhile, the provisional government were making it known that only censored newspapers could be sold and when Charles Eason went to Government Buildings in Upper Merrion Street he was told to cease trading in English papers.

So, what with disorder on the streets and on the railway tracks, staff being unable to get to work and business being curtailed by censorship, it is no wonder that LM Cullen considers the Civil War to have inflicted the most damage on the company.

In 2014, Conor Whelan, then Chief Executive of Eason's, told Tom Lyons of *The Irish Times* of his intention to protect the company's collection of such historical artefacts as Jim Larkin's 1913 letter, demanding that the company stop selling William Martin Murphy's newspapers. There is also the 1886 letter from Charles Eason to WH Smith in which he asks to buy out the company.

Eason's, O'Connell Street, celebrated its 125th birthday in 2011, and writer Dermot Bolger (*b.* 1959) wrote about its importance for Irish writers and customers alike, urging his readers against taking the shop for granted. It is more than a bookshop; it is a historical and social landmark, providing a meeting point for generations of couples whose dates began outside its doors.

Over a hundred and thirty years later, Eason's is one of the stalwarts of O'Connell Street.

THE GENERAL POST OFFICE (GPO)

An *Irish Times* article appeared in October 2019 with the news that the staff in the GPO were to be relocated 'temporarily or permanently' within the year. It quoted an email from Chief Executive David McRedmond, emphasising the urgent need for refurbishment and the enormous cost of that coupled with the fact that the lease was almost run out. Thirty-four years since its last refurbishment, the building was judged by McRedmond to be unfit as a working environment. In conceiving the amount of work

View of GPO and a busy O'Connell Street, c. 1920s–1930s.

required to make it appropriate for a twenty-first-century postal HQ, McRedmond felt that it would be impossible for staff to continue working alongside the construction work that might take many years. In the summer of 2019, the staff were asked for their opinions and the majority elected to stay put, no matter what.

As one of the state's oldest institutions, Ireland's postal service is a couple of hundred years older than the GPO. Dublin's postmaster in the 1640s, Evan Vaughan, established an initial postal service using post boys and horses, who galloped in stages across the island.

After that, we owe the English lord protector Oliver Cromwell (1599–1658) – of all people – for his Postal Act of 1657, which replaced private postal services in Ireland, Scotland and England with a state monopoly.

Another big name associated with the Irish postal service is the novelist

Anthony Trollope (1815–82). The twenty-six-year-old future author of the 'Chronicles of Barsetshire' series arrived at the GPO in 1841, escaping a moneylender and his previous job as a post office clerk in London which he had only just managed to hang onto as he had the habit of playing loose and fast with punctuality and struggled to defer to his superiors. The Irish vacancy – clerk for a postal surveyor in Banagher, County Offaly – could not have come at a better time and proved to be the making of him. In Ireland he found himself a wife, began to write and, all the while, worked his way up through the postal ranks over the following eighteen years until his return to London in 1866. Today, he is also credited with introducing the pillar post box to Britain and Ireland.

A vacant lot on Sackville Street was selected for the build. In the street's previous incarnation as Drogheda Street three houses had stood on the site that the government earmarked for a regiment of soldiers. The story goes that, a short while after the soldiers took up residence, they marched out one morning just before the three houses collapsed. A court case ensued and the space was left empty until 12 August 1814, when the foundation stone for the new GPO was laid by Lord Charles Whitworth (1752–1825), the lord lieutenant, in a grand ceremony that cost £60 – a fraction of the £80,000 price tag for the build itself. The architect Francis Johnston, who had also designed Nelson's Pillar, was responsible for the GPO and he was probably inspired by King's College in Cambridge, as the two buildings share similar attributes, for example, a three-storey exterior along with a triangular portico front and centre offset by three rows of panelled windows. He was probably further inspired by Nelson's Pillar, wanting to build something notable and beautiful to complement that monument. Wicklow granite was used for the 223 x 150-foot (67.97 x 45.72-metre) body while the 80-foot (24-metre) high portico was made of Portland stone. And then there are the six 4 feet 4 inch (1.32 metre) thick Ionic columns that hold up the portico and which Stephen Ferguson, in his book *The GPO:*

1823 drawing by Henry Meyer of Francis Johnston, the architect who designed both the GPO and Nelson's Pillar.

200 Years of History, believes referenced James Gandon's entrance to the House of Lords on the other side of the Liffey.

The GPO opened for business four years after that first stone was laid. Johnston must have been proud of his building as it appears in his portrait painted by TC Thompson (*c.* 1780–1857). Aside from the gratification of seeing his design brought to life, Johnston was presumably thrilled by another feature that alluded to one of his hobbies. Three clocks were mounted beneath the portico, with the central face keeping time, while the other two showed the arrival and departure times of the packet ships. The centrepiece – the main clock – chimed every fifteen minutes, while every hour was celebrated on the hour with a chorus of bells, ranging from one and a half tons to three tons. They rang out for the next sixty-three years until it was discovered that their weight was endangering the building and they had to be removed.

Johnston had achieved what he needed to: a beautiful, functional building that satisfied all his client's professional requirements. The English topographer and novelist James Norris Brewer (*c.* 1777–1839), in the first volume of his 1825 book *The Beauties of Ireland*, used words like 'substantial', 'appropriate' and 'highly ornamental' to describe the GPO. His one quibble was that it was too far from the city's centre. However, he immediately counters this point by declaring that the 'unusual width of the (Sackville) street' more than made up for its remote location.

Business in the GPO could only flourish if it ran like clockwork and this was only possible if the staff were on hand to meet every deadline, no matter the hour. To this end, Johnston was obliged to include accommodation for the staff. In 1826, twenty-eight sorting office clerks were availing of a 'sleeping room' in the GPO. It was spartan living; the 'room' was 9 x 6 feet (2.74 x 1.82 metres) and contained a bed, a jug and a halfpenny candle. The luckier ones had a window.

Meanwhile, the Post Office secretary and his family had the south-east wing of the building at their disposal which they accessed through their own front door on Sackville Street, to the left of the portico.

Sir Edward Smith Lees (1783–1846), his wife Lady Jane and their eight children had enough space within their GPO residence for domestic staff, a servants' hall, kitchen and dressing rooms, including a pantry and cellars in the basement. Stephen Ferguson refers to the Henry Warren picture that celebrates King George IV's arrival in Sackville Street in August 1821.

King George IV visited Sackville Street in August 1821.

In the background, to the left of the portico, Sir Edward's windows are crammed with spectators – presumably his friends and relatives.

Other staff residing in the GPO included Edward Baynes who was responsible for the Penny Post Office, Frederick Homan who ran the British Mail Office, and the minute clerk John Burrowes. These three men lived with their families – Homan and his wife had ten children – in three, four rooms apiece and were also privy to an annual provision of fifteen tons of coal and 218 candles.

But what about the accommodation for female employees? Stephen Ferguson introduces his readers to the GPO housekeeper Anne Draper, whose private quarters in the building were far grander than one might expect. Indeed, they were far grander than Johnston had catered for. His basement plan, drawn up in 1814, marks a single room for the housekeeper in the south-east corner of the GPO, placing her within spitting distance of the female servants. So, how is it that Mrs Draper and her family end up with four rooms, along with her own office on the second floor, right next door to Sir Edward Lees? Furthermore, it seems that, just like her living quarters, her command also extended beyond the usual.

Mrs Draper started working in the GPO in 1814 for £100 a year, the position made vacant by the death of the previous housekeeper. She headed a staff of eight housemaids, two firelighters and two lamplighters.

Disgruntled employee Patrick O'Neill, in his 1831 pamphlet on the Irish Post Office, shared his dislike of the housekeeper with his readers and compared her manner to that of the wife of an Eastern sultan or ruler. He then went on to describe Mr Draper as a quiet and obliging sort of fellow before suggestively complimenting Mrs Draper on her 'ingenuity' to have a door installed where there had been no door before, between her and Sir Edward Lees' apartments, thus enabling them to more efficiently communicate on work matters.

Ferguson reminds us that O'Neill was not the most objective of witnesses.

Postal Secretary Sir Edward Lees enjoyed lavish accommodation in the GPO with his wife, their eight children and servants.

After £30 worth of clothes was stolen from his room, he was not shy in making his complaints to Sir Edward, questioning the flaws in Mrs Draper's empire.

In fact, O'Neill wasn't the only one asking Sir Edward Lees questions. At some point, an enquiry was launched, at the government's behest, into the GPO's expenditure and expenses. Several commissioners did their best to clarify the workings of various financial systems within the GPO. Indeed, when Sir Edward was questioned on 17 October 1823, he showed little understanding himself as we can see in this excerpt:

Examiner: Do you periodically audit that account?

Sir Edward: Never, I never looked at it.

Examiner: Have you ever looked at that account?

Sir Edward: I never have in my life.

A particular sticking point was a fund that had been set up for emergencies and stemmed from fines doled out to staff and contractors whose performance had failed to meet stipulated expectations. By 1823, this fund, which was rarely audited, had amassed a large enough amount to provide all manner of entertainment for Sir Edward and his senior officials. For example, Sir Edward bought himself a new pianoforte and was also able to hire a military band to welcome the Grand Duke Michael of Russia (1798–1849) on his visit to Dublin in 1818. Nobody, it seems, was checking up on how that money was distributed, which allowed for a bit of scope in the spending of it.

Sir Edward was the secretary of the Post Office. His job was to run it in the absence of the Postmaster General, a position that was split between two noblemen who were rarely in Ireland, so it was mostly Sir Edward who was in charge. The GPO administration was sharply criticised in The Ninth Report of the Commissioners, for its 'errors in the Accounts, the frequent embezzlement of private property and the delay and irregularity in the conveyance and delivery of the Mails … so long and loudly complained of by the Public.'

Sir Edward attempted to ignore and resist his superiors' demands to implement improvements. Finally, just when it seemed the only option was to get rid of him, an alternative solution was found, thus enabling Sir Edward to exit the GPO with dignity: Edinburgh's postal secretary Augustus Godby and Sir Edward exchanged post offices.

Each evening at 7pm, the mail coaches left the GPO in great haste for Howth to deliver their load to ships bound for England.

Englishman GR Smith (*b.* 1818) published his memoir about his postal career, *Half-a-Century in the Dead-Letter Office*, in 1908. This office was for letters that could not be initially delivered because of an illegible or inadequate address. For example, one letter was addressed to:

'Mr —,

Little elfet,

Sir Nicolas Dusty School.

The GPO staff interpreted this and sent it on correctly to:

Mr —

St. Nicholas Industrial School,

Little Ilford

Smith visited the GPO in May 1859 to inspect its Dead-Letter department and complimented Sackville Street's Nelson's Column and the GPO. Describing the Irish character as humorous, he repeated a story that was told to him at dinner that first night in Dublin by a fellow postal worker. The man explained how on landing at North Wall, he hailed a jaunty cab to take him to his hotel. Since it was his first time in Dublin, he asked the driver to point out significant buildings and, on Sackville Street, the post office was pointed out to him. Noticing the three statues on the roof, he asked, 'Who are they?'

'Och,' says the driver, 'shure they are the twelve apostles, yer honour.' 'Twelve apostles?' repeats the man. 'But there are only three.' The driver reassures him that the twelve are there but nine of them had been called below to help sort out a backlog of letters. The story is similar to one told earlier suggesting that the cab drivers were used to being asked about the

Postal inspector GR Smith visited the GPO in 1859 and later wrote about his experience in his self-published memoir.

statues and liked to be creative for the tourist.

If 1916 was not a good year for the General Post Office, it cannot be denied that when the Volunteers chose the building and Sackville Street as core locations for what is arguably the most famous rebellion in Irish and British history, they sealed their importance forevermore.

By the time the blazes of Easter 1916 were put out, all that remained of Francis Johnston's original building was the charred façade. Demobbed

The blackened façade of the GPO after the 1916 Rising, with extensive damage to the interior.

soldiers were given the task of ridding the shell of its shattered ninety-eight-year-old interior.

Thanks to the OPW (Office of Public Works), the post-Easter-Rising-War-of-Independence-Civil-War rebuild finally began in earnest in September 1924, on the Henry Street side. Previous proposals about the city's main landmarks included making the Custom House the 'new' GPO and adding a new central train station and port to it. In turn, the old GPO would become the new city hall, while the old city hall and Dublin Castle would be made courts of justice and government offices. In the end, everything stayed the same.

It was a big day for the city when the GPO re-opened for business on Thursday, 11 July 1929. President WT Cosgrave (1880–1965) gave a speech outside the building on a platform erected by the OPW, in which he complimented the build on its Irishness, that is, the material used – the Donegal sandstone and the marble from Kilkenny, Cork and Connemara – and the craftsmen who brought the building back to life. Cosgrave had been stationed in the GPO in 1916 and perhaps this was an emotional moment for him, a moment surely heightened by the sight of the bullet holes in the columns.

The GPO was also the location for Ireland's first radio broadcast in 1916, with equipment 'borrowed' from the Irish School of Wireless Telegraphy a few doors away (now the Grand Central Bar), to announce the Rising in morse code for any passing ships who might spread the word and, thereby, attract international sympathy and help. Nine years later, President Douglas Hyde launched the radio station 2RN in a tiny studio on Denmark Street, emphasising its Irishness with Irish-themed programmes for Irish listeners. In October 1928, the broadcast company de-camped to specially built studios on the fourth floor of the GPO and there they stayed for the next forty years or so until the move to the purpose-built campus in Donnybrook.

The telegraph staff returned to the GPO in April 1932, while secretaries and administrative staff followed a few months later, in October. Finally, following nine years of work, the GPO rebuild reached its successful conclusion in 1933 with a price tag of £276,000.

THE GRESHAM HOTEL

In her memoir *Seventy Years Young*, Lady Fingall (1865–1944) mentions Buswell's Hotel eight times and the Shelbourne twice but does not make a single reference to either Sackville/O'Connell Street or, indeed, the Gresham Hotel.

The fashionable Gresham Hotel stretched over three of the original Georgian houses on Sackville Street.

Meanwhile, Oliver St John Gogarty asks in his memoir, 'What would Dublin do without the Shelbourne?' They obviously did not venture to the north side of the city and avail of all it had to offer, not least the luxury afforded by the Gresham Hotel.

When writer Maria Edgeworth is in need of a cheap hotel on 9 July 1831, she is directed to the Shelbourne Hotel and is appalled by the smell and the dirty room, the barely functioning staff and the awful food.

Contrast their lack of acknowledgment of the Gresham Hotel with Todd Andrews, a young IRA officer who grew up near the Gresham but never, ever imagined that he would be allowed inside it. However, when his boss Emmet Dalton – Michael Collins's right-hand man – established his office in the hotel in 1921–2, Andrews found himself in awe of the 'rich drapes, sumptuous armchairs' and 'deep carpets'; this was a locale that surely jarred with his reasons for being there at all.

A small book was published in 1965, to coincide with the hotel's centenary. Written by Ulick O'Connor (1928–2019), it begins with the revelation that the Gresham Hotel was founded by an Englishman whose life is quite the literal example of a 'rags to riches' story. No date is provided, but when a baby boy was found abandoned on the steps of the Royal Exchange in London, he was named after its founder Sir Thomas Gresham (1519–79). In due course, the infant Thomas grew up and arrived in Dublin, going to work in the home of William Beauman of Rutland Square (now Parnell Square), one of the grandest residential areas at the time and where Thomas rapidly proved himself and was promoted to butler.

In 1817, Thomas left his employer to open a hotel at 21–22 Sackville Street. Ulick O'Connor suspects that this was done with Beauman's help because of a cup inscribed to William in thanks from Gresham and his family. It was a good time to open a hotel as the number of visitors to the city was expanding. From the beginning, Gresham set out to attract a high-class customer. Indeed, 22 Sackville Street had formerly been a lavish home for the Yeates (sometimes, Yates) family, who also owned Moone Abbey in County Kildare. When Gresham bought it, it belonged to John Gardiner, who was probably related to the wealthy Gardiner family. Three years later, Samuel Yeates bought number 20 from George and James Nugent.

A few doors down, at number 25, Jones Hotel was the most popular stopping-off point for coach travellers. Gresham probably took this into consideration when choosing his spot. There were five other hotels on Sackville Street when the Gresham opened for business. However, it must have proved a lucrative and noble investment for its owner since, over the next fifteen years or so, he established himself as a person of worth, becoming president of both the Board of the Agricultural Bank and the Cholera Orphan Society. He was also involved with The Sick and Indigent Room-keepers' Society, Dublin's oldest charity that was set up by seven tradesmen in 1790 to help people in need, no matter their religion.

Goodness only knows how many availed of the hotel's services during that first hundred years. Ulick O'Connor refers to an advertisement from 1870 that proclaimed the Gresham as a favourite with the Imperial French family along with several ex-presidents of America.

For the most part, a hotel provides a location and atmosphere for happy events like brunches, weddings, christenings and Christmas get-togethers. However, on 21 November 1920, during an incident in the War of Independence, two residents were gunned down in their rooms, their blood splattering the walls, furniture and carpets (See page 208).

A few weeks later, Michael Collins's career almost ended in the Gresham. It was Christmas Eve and a private room could not be found so it was decided that the IRA intelligence officers would eat in the main dining room. We can imagine everyone enjoying themselves, eating and drinking the best that the Gresham had to offer until, presumably, the festive mood evaporated with the arrival of British Auxiliaries in search of Collins. When their target tried to leave, he was stopped and searched. The

Michael Collins in the Gresham Hotel sometime in January 1922.

soldiers were armed but all they had was one inadequate photograph of the infamous Michael Collins, obliging Collins to go on the offensive by loudly proclaiming himself as an ordinary, innocent man trying to enjoy his Christmas dinner. He bitterly complained when a soldier actually reached over and ruffled his hair to make him look like the fellow in their photograph. Miraculously, his 'disguise' worked and the soldiers left to search elsewhere.

The Gresham Hotel was obviously a favourite with Collins and his colleagues as, following the announcement of the Truce on 9 July 1921, this was where the IRA met with the British Army to discuss what would happen next.

Less than a year after the Truce was signed, everything fell apart with the outbreak of the Civil War. Michael Collins was living his last weeks, while the Gresham would be severely punished for providing a haven for anti-Treaty Forces. Thursday, 6 July 1922 marks the beginning of the end for Thomas Gresham's construction. At 12.15pm, machine guns focused on the lavish architecture about thirty minutes before two armoured vehicles, crammed with pro-Treaty soldiers, pulled up across the road and aimed their guns at the front door, splintering the walls and shattering the windows. Then came the bombs that created a fire ball. By 1.30pm, the building was tottering and an inferno was spreading due to a southerly breeze. Over the next couple of days five hotels were reduced to rubble: The Gresham, The Hammond, The Granville, The Crown and The Edinburgh, but only one of them would be reborn again.

The reopening of the Gresham Hotel on Saturday, 16 April 1927 caused great excitement, with plenty looking to book rooms and anxious to see its new interior. For people weary of years of war, the sight of this building restored to its former glory must have been a comfort and a clear sign that it was time to move on. Kate Mullen was the new manager, a role she would hold until 1940.

Apart from Thomas Gresham, another important 'T' in the hotel's history is a man after whom the bar is named after. Timothy James ('Toddy') O'Sullivan (1906–94) hailed from Waterville in County Kerry. In 1940, he took over as hotel manager with a Curriculum Vitae that involved managing the Rock Hotel in Gibraltar and the Four Courts Hotel on Ormond Quay, which was demolished in the 1980s to make way for offices. His appointment transformed the hotel as he set about outwitting wartime shortages to ensure that the restaurants and bar continued to provide fulsome fare. To accomplish this, Toddy became something of a 'black market' expert and was obliged to travel miles across Ireland to buy the likes of butter, alcohol and tea.

He employed Karl Uhlemann as head chef and Uhlemann's sous-chef Michael McManus. Both men came from the Regal Rooms, the restaurant attached to the Theatre Royal in Hawkins Street. Born in Alsace-Lorraine, Uhlemann had worked in a variety of restaurants across Europe, Britain and Ireland. During the First World War, he was imprisoned in Oldcastle, County Meath, which proved fruitful since he went on to marry a local girl and never returned to Germany. His reputation was first class and he became governor of the order of merit of the International Academy of Chefs de Cuisine in London.

One of the first changes that Toddy made was to set up a grill room with an extensive à la carte menu. The chefs and the manager were a dream team that triumphed even when British newspaper the *Daily Express* printed one of the à la carte menus on their front page to highlight their disapproval at how prosperous life was in neutral Ireland during wartime. Undoubtedly, plenty of readers agreed with the editor, whilst plenty others treated the coverage as a welcome advertisement for where best to go for delicious food; consequently, hundreds of off-duty British and American servicemen arrived at the hotel in search of the promised land, including ten US airmen with their host First Lady Eleanor Roosevelt (1884–1962).

Less attractive guests were the Irish-based Nazis, who held their 1937

Christmas party in the Aberdeen Room. Two years before the outbreak of the Second World War, this must have been a sight to behold – what with the Swastika flags draped over the balconies and the entire evening being 'overseen' by the huge portrait of Adolf Hitler (1889–1945). Perhaps they raised a glass to the portrait and, led by the German minister to Ireland, Dr Eduard Hempel (1887–1972), serenaded it with the German national anthem, '*Das Lied der Deutschen*', or as it is popularly known, '*Deutschland, Deutschland über alles*'.

Happier memories are to be found in events such as that of 19 December 1909 when that same room was the location for a special lunch organised by the Corinthian Club for Polar explorer Ernest Shackleton (1874–1922). Founder of the gentleman's club and president of the Royal College of Surgeons, Sir Charles Alexander Cameron (1830–1921) gave a speech about the wonder of an Irishman being the greatest of the Antarctic explorers.

Five years after assuming his managerial role, Toddy was made a director of the Gresham Hotel Ltd on 31 August 1945, thus allowing him to implement his grandest plans. Peace had returned and Toddy, wisely anticipating a post-war boom in tourism, set his cap on increasing the number of American visitors who would not baulk at paying good money for excellent service and facilities.

Over the next few years, Toddy built eighty more bedrooms and, furthermore, all rooms were made ensuite – the first Irish hotel to provide this amenity. In 1959, he introduced a Garden Room restaurant. By now the Gresham was the place to be, and on New Year's Eve 1961 the Irish national television broadcasting company, Teilifís Éireann, was launched from the hotel. In the following year, the 34th president of America, President Dwight D Eisenhower (1890–1969), was personally invited by Toddy to visit Ireland. The President came for four days in August 1962, splitting his time between Dublin, Wexford and Wicklow, and of course he stayed at the Gresham with wife, Mamie (1896–1979), and their two grandchildren.

Twenty-five thousand people lined O'Connell Street to bid him farewell as he left the hotel for Wicklow.

In April 1965, Nicholas Pierce, then a young delivery boy, remembers entering the hotel foyer with a stack of new clothes for a fashion show. Unable to see over the pile in his arms, he hurried forward only to find himself well and truly tripped up. Designer clothes hit the floor, as did he. A keen cinema-goer, he immediately recognised the woman fussing over her yappy dogs, whose leads had caused his fall. Elizabeth Taylor (1932–2011) tended to her over-excited pets whilst the stunned Nicholas was helped to his feet by her husband, Richard Burton. The couple lived in the hotel for ten weeks while Burton was filming *The Spy Who Came in from the Cold*, taking over an entire floor with their staff and children. At some point, they shared their penthouse suite with a monkey that took exception to its surroundings and, amongst other things, knocked over precious vases, ripped curtains and the cheek of Taylor's maid. On Saint Patrick's Day, the actress gave every member of staff a baby bottle of Power's Whiskey along with a green carnation.

Other famous visitors included the comedy duo Stan Laurel (1890–1965) and Oliver Hardy (1892–1957), who spent two weeks in the Gresham in May 1952 while performing in the Olympia. In the summer of 1961, royalty descended in the shape of former Hollywood actress and Irish descendant Grace Kelly (1929–82) and her husband Prince Rainier III (1923–2005), a visit which almost ended badly when, following a busy day of appointments, they arrived at the Gresham for a banquet dinner. A five-thousand strong crowd became hysterical and tried to push their way through a struggling cordon of sixty gardaí. The fans screamed, 'We want Grace!' People fainted; children were crushed and one woman may even have had a heart attack. It was reported that as many as fifty were treated by ambulance crews. Order was finally regained, although the prince and princess looked notably upset as they entered the hotel. However, the crowd were rewarded when Princess

Grace Kelly about to embark on the ocean liner Constitution *to marry Prince Rainier, 1956.*

Grace appeared on the Gresham's balcony, waving and smiling once more.

In 1963, the Beatles had to be delivered to the hotel in an *Evening Herald* van for their night's stay, following their electrifying concert in the Adelphi Cinema on 7 November. For safety reasons, they were brought through the kitchen, much to the delight of the staff who never normally got within earshot of important guests.

Queen of Jazz Ella Fitzgerald (1917–96) stayed in the Gresham in April 1964 for her performance at the Adelphi. In 1967, singer and legendary trumpet player Louis Armstrong (1901–71) also chose the hotel as his base while staging two sold-out concerts at the Adelphi. On 8 July 1974, American actor and film maker John Wayne (1907–79) stayed in the Gresham and, the following morning, breakfasted on two fried eggs, half a dozen rashers, sausages, tea and toast while happily agreeing to be interviewed by Paddy Murray (*b*. 1953), a young journalist from the *Evening Herald* who had presented himself at the movie star's table. Amongst other things, Wayne spoke of his admiration for President Richard Nixon (1913–94) and his belief in the President's innocence just weeks before Nixon resigned the presidency on 9 August. Wayne asked Murray where he might purchase a báinín hat (knitted peak hat) and blackthorn stick, and after breakfast, Murray and his photographer walked him to the souvenir shop (now the site of Toddy's Bar) to do his shopping.

Toddy O'Sullivan lived with his wife Niamh and their two children in a penthouse apartment on the fifth floor of the hotel. By all accounts, they made a wonderful partnership in running the hotel together as well as being hugely popular in an A-list celebrity world. It was quite a thing to be invited into their home. One friend, a return visitor to the hotel, was Emmet Dalton, Michael Collin's right-hand man who had been with him when he died. Dalton had been based at the Gresham during the heady years of 1921–2 and, thirty years later, was to be found living in London with his wife Alice, involved in making films.

John Wayne, on the left, during the filming of The Quiet Man *in Cong in County Mayo. His Irish tweed cap was a variation on a style commonly worn in Ireland at the time and after the success of the movie it became the height of fashion.*

The Daltons were frequent visitors to Ireland, with the aim of developing Ireland's Ardmore film studios and they always stayed in the Gresham. When Alice died unexpectedly at their Kensington house on 1 September 1957 her husband wanted to bury her in Glasnevin Cemetery in Dublin. After the London funeral, the grieving family boarded a plane to Dublin and were met by Toddy O'Sullivan who drove them back to the Gresham.

Toddy finally retired in 1968 and moved out to 'Ballycarbery' in Killiney,

Emmet Dalton and his wife Alice were good friends with the Gresham Hotel's manager Toddy O'Sullivan.

although he remained a deputy chairman of the Gresham Hotel Ltd. By then, it is fair to say that his and the hotel's 'golden age' had faded. Throughout the 1960s it was listed by Egon Ronay as one of Dublin's top hotels, but towards the end of the decade it was losing its place amidst stiff competition. It would seem that its heyday of accommodating 80,000 guests annually, thanks to a legion of 400 staff, was over. Undoubtedly the falling figures signalled a growing attraction for holidaying outside of Ireland. In the early 1970s, it became part of the Ryan Hotel Group and ran into difficulties with staffing and the unions.

Today, however, it appears to have righted its crown once more after finding new owners in 2016, Spain's Riu hotel group, who paid out €92 million for it. With a new name, Riu Plaza The Gresham Hotel, it is proving once more a worthy investment, with a seventeen per cent rise in profits. Now employing an approximate 153 staff, the hotel boasts 323 rooms and suites, twenty function rooms, a restaurant and, of course, the very comfortable Toddy's Bar.

THE HAPPY RING HOUSE

McDowell's Jewellers – or its preferred name, the Happy Ring House – is one of the longest-running family businesses on O'Connell Street.

Originally from Cavan, John McDowell (*b.* 1839) opened his 'Practical Watchmaker and Jeweller's shop' at 19 Mary Street in 1870, at some point handing over the running of the shop to his younger brother William (1857–1939). The shop received a glowing review in the 1887 book *Industries of Dublin*, in which it was described as being 'one of the most attractive shops in Mary Street'. The review also commented on its spaciousness – 25 x 45 feet (7.62 x 13.7 metres) – which allowed McDowell to have his product manufactured alongside the salesroom, ensuring a natural efficiency for supply and demand.

The staff totalled six and the selection on offer included clocks of all shapes and sizes, watches and rings. Even back then they were known as specialists when it came to wedding rings – and guard rings, which was a ring worn to hold another in place, thereby preventing it from slipping off the finger. Also available were brooches, earrings, studs, snuff-boxes, perfume and card cases, gold, silver, and hair chains (gold or silver chains that ladies wore, like necklaces, in their hair).

Their prices were very competitive, while particular mention was made of Mr McDowell's speciality in working with Connemara marble.

The 1901 Census records show the forty-eight-year-old John McDowell

The Happy Ring House is one of the longest running family businesses on O'Connell Street.

living at 3 Sackville Street with his fifty-year-old wife, Harriet, and his thirty-year-old brother William, a bachelor, in their home that is described as a shop/dwelling. A year later, the McDowells left their Mary Street premises to set up the store on Sackville Street.

The business thrived, and ten years later, the 1911 Census records John as retired and living in Howth with Harriet, providing a home for John's sister and her two American-born children.

Meanwhile, the same census shows the forty-nine-year-old William, jeweller, now married five years to twenty-five-year-old Caroline from Meath. The couple had two children and lived in Sackville Street. Fifteen years later, the shop fell victim to the Rising twice over, first looted and then bombarded by the *Helga* gunboat and burnt to the ground.

In 2016, William's grandson Peter was interviewed for an article in the *Irish Independent* about family businesses that had survived the Rising and were still going strong. Peter McDowell explained how his grandfather remained in the shop to prevent looting until it became too dangerous. In the midst of the chaos, William and the porter made a risky run from the shop to Cathedral Street. Only William survived the dash to safety, although he was wounded, with a bullet in his leg.

Rebuilding began as soon as possible and, in 1917, contractor Francis Bergin (1855–1925), an experienced railway engineer, actually used girders salvaged from the ruins of the GPO in the reconstruction of the McDowell premises. Furthermore, William was reimbursed for his looted stock.

Shift forward to 1935, which kickstarted an era of much prosperity when the shop was in the care of William's son Jack McDowell. Jack's name crops up in relation to the infamous 1947 Aintree Grand National. He had bought a horse for 50 guineas from Fingal, County Dublin as a present for his mother and entered it into the most famous national hunt race in the business. The horse was named *Caughoo*, after the Cavan village that the McDowells hailed from.

The story goes that Jack bought the gelding with his brother Herbert, a vet, for 50 guineas, and it was Herbert who trained him at Wheatfield in Malahide. Initially, it seemed that the horse was a dud, being small and unsociable and showing little aptitude for running on the flat or jumping obstacles. However, Herbert's faith was rewarded when *Caughoo* won the Ulster Grand National in 1945 and 1946. No matter, the horse was mostly unknown to the betting crowds that gathered in Aintree on Saturday, 29 March 1947, and the odds on him winning the prestigious race were placed at a hundred to one.

His jockey was also unknown. Eddie Dempsey (1911–89), a thirty-six-year-old national hunt jockey from Meath, had just one win under his belt, the 1941 Enniskerry Hurdle in the Phoenix Park, on the horse *Prince Regent*. This was also Eddie's first visit to England.

On the boat to Liverpool, racing photographer Billy Merriman bumped into Jack McDowell who told him to put a bet on his horse as it was going to win the Grand National.

Meanwhile, in County Clare, eighty-three-year-old farmer John Mungovan had a dream in which two men were discussing who would win the Grand National. One of them chose *Prince Regent*, while the other declared that '*Caughoo* will run away with it!' The morning of the race, the farmer read the list of participants and *Caughoo*'s name jumped out at him. He went and placed a £30 bet on *Caughoo* at his local book-ies, who laughed when John Mundovan warned that he would be taking money from them.

You can watch the race on YouTube, where clarity is poor thanks to outdated technology but also thanks to a fog that hung over the racecourse. It had rained heavily that morning and was followed by a fog that was so thick it was thought that the race might be postponed.

The commentator's voice, at least, is perfectly clear, though he too must have been challenged by the poor visibility. Fifty-seven horses lined up – the biggest number to take part in the race since 1929 – but only nineteen would complete the twenty laps; mercifully, there were no fatalities. It was an Irish win, no matter which way you look at it. For the first three min-utes, the leader is another Irish horse, *Lough Conn*, who is being ridden by Eddie Dempsey's friend Donal McCann. Then, 'from nowhere', to quote the commentator, the unknown *Caughoo* appears briefly alongside *Lough Conn* before moving ahead to take the lead.

As a total of twenty-six horses approach the final jump, *Caughoo*,

Caughoo and jockey E Dempsey after their Grand National win.

described as 'an unknown Irish horse', is well out in front and prevails to take an easy win, netting the McDowells £10,000. The story goes that the win was so unexpected that it silenced the 100,000-strong audience in the stands. Meanwhile, back in Dublin, *Caughoo* was so heavily backed by punters that a local bookie went bankrupt. When Jack McDowell heard this, he paid out and set the bookie back in business once more.

Following the race, an elated Jack McDowell took the ferry back to Ireland and celebrated in style. He approached the barman and asked him to guess the price of his stock, before giving him a cheque for £200, which also ensured the barman a good tip. In other words, he ordered the entire contents of the bar on the SS *Slievemore* in a single round, an act which brought him another win. This time, he ended up in the *Guinness Book of Records* for buying the largest round of drinks ever. Even so, the glasses were empty long before the SS *Slievemore* docked in at Dublin's North Wall, where crowds were waiting to greet and accompany an impromptu parade down O'Connell Street.

Meanwhile, when Eddie Dempsey got home to Ashbourne, he threw a party that drained the local pubs of every drop of alcohol. Down in Clare, Farmer Mungoven's £30 bet nabbed him £3,000. He gave a third of it to the Bishop of Killaloe, asking that it be forwarded on to the pope for the relief of distress in Europe.

Uproar ensued a few years later in 1955, when Donal McCann, who came in second on *Lough Conn*, bumped into Eddie Dempsey in a bar and, after a few drinks, accused him of hiding *Caughoo* in the fog to run just one circuit of the course, therefore only making half the jumps. Dempsey was badly beaten up by McCann who ended up in jail for four months. McCann persisted with his theory and actually brought Dempsey to court over the matter, declaring that Dempsey had 'lingered' at the twelfth jump on the first lap until his fellow competitors came around for the second lap. The judge was not convinced and the court case was Eddie's last win. Following his retirement in 1950, he was in need of money and sold his story to a Sunday tabloid, saying that he had cheated by hiding himself and *Caughoo* behind a haystack. However, there were no haystacks that day.

It was *Caughoo's* final win, although he did become something of a celebrity in Malahide where he died in 1961.

In 1999, *The Daily Mirror* ran a story that proved *Caughoo* to be the legitimate winner in 1947, after obtaining two different photographs of *Caughoo* making the jump at Becher's Brook, the most famous fence on the Grand National circuit thanks to its sheer size. Peter McDowell was interviewed and shared his relief at the horse's name and jockey being finally cleared of cheating. The article also referred to yet another controversy associated with *Caughoo*.

The horse was buried in Malahide, but his head supposedly had been given to a Dublin taxidermist firm. It was never collected and then the firm was disbanded after the owner died. All the items were sold off and an apprentice taxidermist ended up with the head. At some point, he met up with Frank Godfrey, former mayor of Drogheda, and told him he had the head of the 1947 Grand National victor. The taxidermist told how every year he would place the head alongside him, with a bottle of stout, to watch the Grand National. Godfrey persuaded the man to part with the head for £80 and brought it home to Donore. Eddie Dempsey visited Donore in 1986 and had his photograph taken with the head, promising that he and *Caughoo* had completed the entire race and that the win was genuine – although whether the head had belonged to *Caughoo* continued to be the subject of much debate.

Jack McDowell was the man behind the famous cinema advertisement for the Happy Ring House. According to Peter McDowell, the company decided to target young couples on a typical night out, who might meet up at Nelson's Pillar, have a meal in a nearby restaurant and then go see a film.

As a happy consequence of the Happy Ring House's speedy recognition of the benefits of onscreen advertising the jewellers were able to monopolise the cinema screen from the mid-1950s to the early 1970s. This was also due to the fact that Cinema and General Publicity (CGP), who controlled advertising in the city's cinemas, stipulated that only one advertisement could be allowed per sector.

When asked if the cinema advert provided a boost in business, Peter McDowell explained that while no big surge in profits was felt, the Happy Ring House was always aware of other jewellers in the wings waiting for their spot on the screen.

Cinema and General Publicity produced the adverts, only requiring the Happy Ring House to contribute its logo.

When the mass production of affordable television sets took its toll on cinema audiences, the Happy Ring House was, once again, the first of its sector to react, becoming the first Irish jewellers to advertise on the TV screen.

Above: The Savoy is Dublin's oldest cinema.
Below: The Savoy under construction in 1928.

CHAPTER FOUR

The Cinemas

THE SAVOY

The Savoy is the oldest cinema in Dublin and, like most of the landmark buildings on O'Connell Street, it was once very beautiful, inside and out. Built on the site of the former Granville Hotel, one of several unfortunate businesses that were permanently lost in the rubble of the Civil War, it was designed by architect Londoner Frederick Charles Mitchell and built by Meagher & Hayes for Associate Irish Cinemas, the Irish division of Associated British Cinemas, and opened in 1929.

Portland stone was the material of choice, while the exterior imitated the Classical style, perhaps to complement its neighbour the Gresham Hotel.

Inside, the customer was encouraged to forget about the busy street outside thanks to a Venetian-inspired interior. The huge safety curtain provided a luxurious canvas for a painting of the Doge's Palace, while the stage was topped by a spectacular arch that replicated Venice's Bridge of Sighs and the walls were decorated with painted Venetian windows and balconies. The intention was to induce a special atmosphere, which it surely did.

The Savoy's interior did its best to convince customers that they were actually in Venice.

One can imagine hushed voices and feelings of sheer elation as those very first customers made their way inside to be the first person to sit in their seat. It certainly looked and felt theatrical, and that first audience might well have been distracted and thrilled by the sheer size of the building that included stage facilities and 2,789 seats. It cost £200,000, which included the £10,000 price tag of the three state-of-the-art Ross projectors. Apart from the actual cinema space, the Savoy provided a cloakroom, telephone kiosks and a restaurant, while elevators were also available to access each floor. If restaurant fare did not appeal, each film had an intermission to allow for the buying of sweets, chocolate and ice-cream.

President WT Cosgrave presided over the grand opening on 29 November 1929, and it seems fitting that the first film shown was Alan Crosland's (1894–1936) ground-breaking musical, the natural colour and all-singing *On With the Show!*, starring a large cast who have mostly been forgotten today, including twins Marion (1900–73) and Madeleine Fairbanks (1900–89). Released by Warner Bros in 1929, the Savoy's very first film was Warner's first all-talking, all-colour feature length film and would prove a world-wide box office hit.

However, there was one film that would break all the records and that was David O Selznick's (1902–65) lavish production of Margaret Mitchell's (1900–49) 1936 novel, *Gone with the Wind*. It arrived at the Savoy in 1939 and over the course of its eight weeks' residency it was seen by approximately 300,000 people. That same year, the cinema was sold to the independent Elliman Group, whose hold was temporary as it was taken over by Odeon (Ireland) Ltd in 1946.

Two months after it opened, the Savoy found itself hosting a cultural spat when it showed the American silent film, *Smiling Irish Eyes*, which proved as patronising as it sounds and offended plenty. In the book *Cinema and Ireland*, Kevin Rockett quotes Mary Manning's review of the film in *The New Statesman*, where she calls the film the worst that was ever made. The manager of the Savoy claimed that his staff had cut out the very worst bits, but this was not enough to prevent a veritable mutiny. Its reputation had preceded it, resulting in a group of rowdy students – including future actor Cyril Cusack, future film-maker Liam O'Leary (1910–92) and a future president of Ireland Cearbhall Ó Dálaigh (1911–78) – storming the Savoy on *Smiling Irish Eyes'* first night. Once inside, they provided

Smiling Irish Eyes' *film poster.*

a running commentary for the silent film, shouting out lines like 'It's an insult!' and 'Take it off!' Inevitably, the projector came to a halt and F Knott, the Savoy's manager, an Englishman, appeared on stage in an attempt to rouse sympathy for his cause by lamenting about the students breaking into his cinema. This was met by the blunt retort, 'You have broken into our country!' Then, the crowd broke into song. Knott's solution was to promise solemnly that he would organise a meeting with his superiors about getting rid of the film but, in the meantime, could he not continue to show it and, as soon as it was over, he would ask for a show of hands to see what the rest of the audience thought of it? Unimpressed, the students informed him that he was asking Irish people to vote about their being Irish or stage-Irish.

Trouble of a similar nature brewed again in December 1934 when the Savoy showed the wedding of Prince George, the new Duke of Kent (1902–42) and Princess Marina of Greece and Denmark (1906–68). Only engaged since August, their wedding was the first royal wedding to be organised as a media spectacle – the endgame to create loyalty to the crown. In the Savoy, the response fell somewhat short of that desire when fifty protestors waited for the film to start and then directed their anger at the screen. Some threw ink over it, whilst others tore off as much as they could.

In 2005, former employee Herbie Donnelly (1925–2018) was interviewed by *The Irish Times* film critic Donald Clarke. He was nineteen when he accepted the position of senior usher in 1944, for £3.10.0 a week, which he said was good money for the time. He remembers the organist playing before every film, the words of the song appearing on the screen to allow the audience to sing along. Donnelly described the wonder of listening to over 2,000 people singing out from their seats. Back then, people dressed up to go to the cinema, including the staff. Donnelly declared that he struck quite a pose in his usher's uniform, comparing himself to the guards outside Buckingham Palace. His job was to police the queues and be ready to expel any troublemakers. He told how he always ushered expectant mothers ahead because he did not believe in making them stand in line.

Donnelly worked in the Savoy until 1947 when he was transferred to the Theatre Royal. Many years later, a woman approached him and asked him if he had worked in the Savoy. When he said yes, she gifted him a box of cigarettes for allowing her entrance ahead of a long queue when she was pregnant with her son, who was now a strapping sixteen-year-old.

Before leaving the Savoy in 1947, Donnelly worked the night of the big storm, the subject of Kevin Kearns's book *Ireland's Arctic Siege: The Big Freeze of 1947*. It was Sunday, 12 January and the long queue outside the Savoy was for the next showing of Alfred Hitchcock's (1899–1980) *Spellbound*, starring Gregory Peck (1916–2003) and Ingrid Bergman (1915–82). Meanwhile, inside, the film was playing to a full house. The weather was wet and dismal, but things took a nasty turn between 5 and 6pm when a ferocious storm of winds and torrential rain struck O'Connell Street. Inside the cinema, a blissfully ignorant audience were glued to the screen until the electricity went, sometime after 6pm, throwing the huge auditorium into darkness. The blackout was caused by strong winds, bringing down ESB lines, and lasting six hours. Donnelly and his colleagues had to lead over 2,000 patrons out of the building by torchlight and see them off into the hellish weather. The entire city was in darkness, with hundreds having to make their way home from cinemas, theatres and restaurants using the lights from passing cars and buses.

With business booming, the Savoy underwent the first of its many alterations when Ireland's first CinemaScope screen was introduced in time to show the 1953 biblical epic – and Ireland's first widescreen film – *The Robe*, starring Richard Burton (1925–84) and Jean Simmons (1929–2010).

In 1960, the Rank Organisation dismantled the Venetian theme, replacing it with a more contemporary look.

The first of several renovations took place over six months in 1969 when £400,000 was spent dividing the cinema into two screens. Six years later, the restaurant was replaced with a 200-seater cinema. Two more were added by 1979 and a sixth screen was squeezed in, in 1988. The new builds saw the cinema sacrifice a third of its initial capacity.

Rumours circulated in February 2012 that the Savoy might have to close its doors, with audiences falling from 740,000 a year to 250,000.

A seventh screen, an Advance Screening Room, was added in 2014, two years before Screen Two and its 500 seats were broken up into three smaller screens, giving the Savoy a total of nine screens. It was perhaps inevitable that Screen One, which could seat 750, was divided up in 2018. In fact, this decision to split the iconic Screen One into five smaller cinemas, was a result of months of discussion and debate for its owners IMC and it proved unpopular with many cinema-goers including RTÉ presenter Rick O'Shea (b. 1973); he protested at the loss of such a classic cinema space, a throwback to the golden age of cinema. A generation of Dubliners flocked to Screen One in 1977 to see the first of the George Lucas (b. 1944) *Star Wars* trilogy. Many film fans will surely remember the lengthy queues for hotly anticipated films and then, the audience applauding as the final credits rolled. Screen One was a favourite because this was where the big new releases were shown.

The Savoy has hosted many film premiers, including the 1991 European premier of Alan Parker's (1944–2020) *The Commitments*. One of the highlights in the cinema's history was the second John Ford Ireland Symposium that took place in 2013, at which the seventy-three-year-old Patrick, son of John Wayne, spoke about his father's and his godfather's, John Ford (1894–1973), love for Ireland and the making of the hugely popular *The Quiet Man*.

In 1985, the Irish Architectural Archive obtained something very special indeed, an album containing twenty-five photographs, taken between July 1928 and January 1930, which chart the construction of the Savoy and can be viewed at https://digital.ucd.ie/view/ucdlib:45872.

THE CARLTON

The Carlton, at 52–54 Sackville Street, was the last of several new cinemas that opened in 1915. It was launched just after Christmas, on 27 December, with the black-and-white silent film *His Wife's Story*, which was accompanied by a small orchestra comprised of musicians playing two violins, a piano and a cello.

Architect Thomas F McNamara's design and layout received complimentary notices in the *Bioscope*, the British cinema trade journal. 'Paddy', the Irish correspondent, noted the lavish entrance and tearoom, which was also a lounge, praising the lighting, the slope in the floor and the generous proportions of the main hall, while *The Irish Times* declared that Carlton customers would never be faced with a breakdown thanks to the expensive projectors and generators. The man behind the Carlton, Frank W Chambers, also ran a tobacconist and billiards hall nearby.

It proved a great favourite with Dubliners, offering not just the latest film, but also musical performances, which was an achievement considering it had to compete with the likes of the Rotunda and the Bohemian Picture Theatre.

Frank Chambers did not stay long, abandoning the Carlton for the much bigger and grander La Scala which opened in August 1920 and boasted 3,200 seats.

The Carlton was forced to close in 1936 due to accumulated damages it sustained during the Easter Rising and the Civil War. In 1937, three different promoters, McCabe, Robinson and Ellis, banded together and bought the building and its immediate neighbours. Architects Robinson & Keefe built the new Carlton in the Art Deco style that had originated in Paris in the 1920s and signalled post-war celebration and glamorous craftsmanship through furniture, architecture, jewellery, fashion and cinema houses. There were 2,000 seats in all, 1,500 in the stalls and 500 in the circle, along with a stage and dressing room. Following two years of renovation, it re-opened for business on 16 April 1938 with a Cary Grant (1904–86) film, *The Awful Truth*. The first week was a successful one with 32,000 customers, and the café and restaurant proved especially popular.

In 1956, it hosted the European premier of the musical *Rock Around the Clock*. Featuring Bill Hailey (1925–81) and his Comets, amongst others, and created to capitalise on the massive success of the bestselling song, the film was a huge hit and a grand total of 97,000 rock 'n' roll fans packed out the Carlton for three weeks.

The artist Robert Ballagh was thirteen years of age when the film opened in Ireland. His father brought him to the Carlton, where they were both surprised to see several gardaí posted outside. Ballagh describes how the film had barely flickered into being on the screen when an assorted mix of Teddy Boys, their partners and other brave souls jumped into the aisles and furiously jived and jitterbugged until the final credits rolled. The Carlton was appreciated for action – that is, action films such as westerns, slapstick comedies and horrors.

The cinema changed hands in 1959 when it was sold to a new company, Adelphi-Carlton Ltd, a subsidiary of Associated British Cinemas (ABC). It was sold on again in the late 1960s when EMI took it over. Under their influence, the 1970s saw the cinema make good use of its stage with a string of sell-out concerts from world-class artists like Duke Ellington (1899–1974), just before his death on 24 May and Johnny Cash (1932–2003), who played two nights in 1975.

In 1976, the 2,000-seater was divided into three screens. Later on, the once-popular restaurant was replaced by a fourth screen. At one point, the cinema was nicknamed the 'House of Horror' on account of its loyalty to that genre. Unfortunately, it wouldn't last another twenty years and Dubliners were obliged to say goodbye to the Carlton Cinema in October 1994. Its final two films were a throwback to its heyday: *Singin' in the Rain* and *Rock Around the Clock*. RTÉ's Colm Connolly reported on the closure, referring to the cinema as a Dublin institution and landmark. He interviewed usher Paddy Short who lamented the loss of so many of O'Connell Street's cinemas, including the Metropole, Ambassador and the Grand Central. Colm Connolly was obliged to repeat his report in November of the following year, this time announcing the closure of the Carlton's sister cinema, the Adelphi, in Middle Abbey Street, which was being knocked down to make way for a carpark. The Carlton was spared such a fate thanks to its 1916 connections, though the building generated years of disagreements over what was to be done with it. Today, the façade still reflects the Art Deco theme, which some may feel appropriate for its new host, the Carlton Casino Club.

THE METROPOLE CINEMA AND RESTAURANT

The Metropole Cinema and Restaurant opened on 9 February 1922 with the 1921 silent film *Peck's Bad Boy*, starring Jackie Coogan (1914–84). It rose out of the ashes of the Metropole Hotel, which had had its own garrison during the Easter Rising and had been destroyed due to its proximity to the GPO.

The hotel, previously four separate Georgian buildings, had been one of the most popular in Dublin for those who could afford to stay in one of its hundred rooms. In fact, that Easter Monday, 24 April, when leaders of the Rising James Connolly (1868–1916) and Pádraig Pearse (1879–1916) led their men up Sackville Street, there were several British officers staying in the hotel who gradually found themselves completely caught off guard.

The Adelphi Cinema opened on Middle Abbey Street in 1939 and was knocked down in 1995 to make way for a carpark.

James Connolly put Lieutenant Oscar Traynor (1886–1963) in command of the Metropole garrison, who must have congratulated themselves on being assigned to such a pleasant location. The group of young insurgents had little to do in the hotel aside from appreciating the first-class facilities and chatting, via the bedroom windows, with their colleagues in the GPO.

The hotel's demise was begun in earnest on Thursday, 27 April when Traynor removed his men to the post office after the hotel was fired on. Pádraig Pearse, however, queried their evacuating their position because of a few shells and sent them back again. Another twenty-four hours passed and the hotel was taking a severe battering from a cannon that had been placed on Parnell Square and was – presumably – aiming for the post office but kept missing its target. This time, Traynor's squadron left never to return. Smoking rubble was all that was left of this magnificent hotel

The beautiful Metropole Hotel was destroyed during Easter week 1916.

by the time Pearse surrendered.

Designed by Drumcondra-born architect Aubrey V O'Rourke (1885–1928), the new Metropole cinema and restaurant was a five-storey building that surely heralded the coming of the big entertainment complexes. Like most of the buildings on O'Connell Street, the style was a sort of minimalist, classical look. In all, it provided 200 Dubliners with a job. Apart from a 1,000-seater cinema, grill-room and restaurant, it included a bar and a ballroom that faced onto O'Connell Street. O'Rourke had two other cinema houses to his name, the Phibsboro Cinema and the Pillar Picture House, which also had an O'Connell Street address.

Much smaller than the Metropole and formerly a block of offices, the Pillar Picture House opened on 2 December 1914. Bookended by two World Wars, it had a good run of thirty years before closing on 25 May 1945.

The English playwright William Shakespeare (1564–1616) provided the inspiration for the Metropole's interior, whose walls were adorned with paintings of scenes from his plays.

THE ILLUSTRATED
SPORTING & DRAMATIC
NEWS

No. 2,166.—Vol. LXXXIII. [REGISTERED FOR TRANSMISSION IN THE UNITED KINGDOM] SATURDAY, MARCH 20, 1915. PRICE SIXPENCE, By Post, 6½d.

"RANJI" OUT!—AT THE FRONT.
MAJOR H.H. RANJITSINHJI, JAMSAHEB OF NAWANAGAR, WHO IS SERVING WITH THE INDIAN CAVALRY IN FRANCE.

Prince Ranjitsinhji played cricket for England and was invited to visit Ireland by President WT Cosgrave.

Writer Oliver St John Gogarty described attending a huge party at the Metropole in the summer of 1924, in aid of the Tailtean Games, the Irish Free State's version of the Olympics that ran from 1924 to 1932. He was one of 1,000 guests and the guest of honour was His Highness Prince Ranjitsinhji (1872–1933) of Nawangar, who was the first non-white player to play for England's cricket team. The previous year, the prince had attended the Assembly of the League of Nations in Geneva, where he met the Irish delegation and was invited to come to Ireland by President WT Cosgrave. Gogarty describes the cricketer as looking 'magnificent in his jewelled turban'. Governor-General Tim Healy (1855–1931) made the opening speech, and Gogarty envied his friend's composure and ability to command such a large audience from the get-go.

The Metropole was taken over by the Rank Organisation in the 1950s and showed all the greats, from *Lawrence of Arabia* (1963) to *Doctor Zhivago* (1965). In his autobiography *Just Joe*, RTÉ broadcaster Joe Duffy (*b.* 1956) reminisces about his 1969 summer job in the Metropole as a thirteen-year-old bellboy when it seemed to him that *Doctor Zhivago* was played constantly. The ballroom was on the second floor and Duffy remembers Ritchie Burbridge and his orchestra performing for the frequent 'dress dances'. The dances made him a small fortune in tips as he ferried thirsty husbands and boyfriends in his elevator from the second floor down to the Long Bar in the basement for a sneaky pint.

The Metropole lasted fifty-one years, closing its doors on 11 March 1972, when it was sold on to the British Home Stores company, who promptly demolished the beautiful building and replaced it with their department store. Twenty years later, BHS gave way to Penneys in 1992. Writer Dermot Bolger (*b.* 1959), in his 2014 article 'O'Connell Street: Where the Street Has No Shame', for *Independent.ie*, lamented the loss of the Metropole, which he described as 'the beating heart' of 1940s O'Connell Street. He added that when director Niall Jordan (*b.* 1950) was making his film *Michael Collins* in the 1990s, he preferred to build a replica of the GPO rather than allow its ugly neighbour intrude upon the screen as the film was set in the early 1900s, when most of Sackville Street was a showcase for gorgeous architecture. His sentiments were echoed by Senator David Norris (*b.* 1944), whose outcry, in 2014, was, 'What kind of street is this for a capital city in the twenty-first century?'

THE GRAND CENTRAL CINEMA

The Grand Central Cinema, with 800 seats, opened in 1921. Its owner Alderman John J Farrell already had several cinemas to his name, including the 370-seater The Pillar Picture House at 62 Upper O'Connell Street. He named his cinema after the original Grand Central Cinema, which had stood next door to the previous tenant of the site, the Dublin Bread Company, before they were both swallowed up in the flames of 1916.

A strong head for heights was required to navigate the new cinema's steep balcony that caused vertigo for some of its customers. Built in the Neo-Classical style, the building was fronted by a decorative archway, a large canopy made of glass and steel, which kept queuing customers relatively sheltered from inclement weather. However, it must have been a challenge to make a profit as there were so many cinemas within walking distance, including the glamorous Metropole and the massive La Scala cinema in Prince's Street. The Grand Central was damaged by a Civil War bomb in 1923 but managed to survive until 1946, when it finally met its end, just like its predecessor, as the result of a fire caused by a violent electrical storm. In the 1940s the building was reopened as a bank.

LA SCALA THEATRE AND OPERA HOUSE

La Scala Theatre and Opera House opened for business on 10 August 1920, on the site which had previously held the offices of the *Freeman's Journal*, just off O'Connell Street. Known as Dublin's new 'super' cinema, it was a 1,900-seater with two balconies and thirty-two private boxes. An early reference to it in Ireland's first film magazine, the *Irish Limelight*, in 1918 promised that it would have more seats than the Gaiety Theatre. Perhaps the grand title was somewhat misleading for a cinema. However, like its immediate neighbour the Metropole, it included a restaurant, lounge, café and ballroom. Designed in the Edwardian style by architect Thomas F McNamara (1867–1947), it was named after the famous opera house in Milan, Italy. The foyer had a marble floor and the walls were lined with wooden panels; both floor and panels came from the *Mauretania*, the sister ship of the ill-fated *Lusitania*, torpedoed in 1915 by a German submarine eleven miles off Kinsale, with the loss of 1,198 souls.

In 1923, the theatre hosted the World Light Heavyweight and the European Championship, on St Patrick's night, between Clare-born Irish American Mike McTigue (1892–1966) and the defending World and European champion Ahmadou M'barick Fall from Senegal, otherwise known as the Battling Siki (1897–1925).

In fact, it should have taken place in Britain, but the World Champion was refused entry because of the colour of his skin. So, the newly independent Irish Free State offered its services. This was a complicated risk for all concerned as the country was caught up in a vicious civil war. Republicans, who opposed the 1921 Treaty, wanted a clamp down on sporting and social gatherings to protest the harsh treatment of IRA prisoners by the pro-Treaty authorities.

Three days before the fight, Republicans declared the nation to be in mourning and, therefore, all sporting and entertainment events were cancelled. But there was big money to be made in an international event such as this. Over 300 journalists from all over the world had applied for press passes. It would be a coup d'état if the IRA could squelch this hugely anticipated boxing match and, similarly, the Free State government could not afford to lose face on such a public stage and were determined it should go ahead.

On St Patrick's morning, the manager of the La Scala received a hand-written note telling him that if the fight went ahead, there would be serious consequences. Minister for Justice Kevin O'Higgins (1892–1927) promised 'ample protection' for the theatre.

Later that day, 500 Free State guards, and armoured cars, took up position around Sackville and Prince's Street. Meanwhile, apart from the 30,000-strong crowd that gathered outside the theatre, the event was endorsed by the presence of both the Minister of Trade and Commerce, Joseph McGrath (1888–1966), and the Attorney General, Hugh Edward Kennedy KC (1879–1936).

Still, the IRA made their move, but their attempt

Light heavyweight boxer 'Bold' Mike McTigue (pictured above left) and his 1923 opponent, World and European champion Ahmadou M'barick Fall, 'Battling Siki' (pictured on the right below).

to blow up the power cables at Henry Place produced nothing more than a big bang. The fight went ahead, and twenty rounds later McTigue was declared the new champion, making him the first Irishman to win a world title on Irish soil.

One hopes he savoured the moment as both his and Siki's fortunes deteriorated after this match. Siki, who had enjoyed his Irish visit, complained that the referee was biased against him and swore off fighting in a foreign ring. He changed his mind after moving to America but failed to ignite his career. Two years later, his body was found, a bullet in his back, in Hell's Kitchen, New York. He was just twenty-eight years old.

Mike McTigue returned to New York and failed to repeat his La Scala success, finally retiring from boxing at thirty-eight years of age, whereupon he opened up an initially successful bar in Long Island that ran aground in the late 1940s. He spent the last few years of his life in a losing battle against poverty and mental health problems and died in a mental institution in 1966.

THE CAPITOL

In 1927, Paramount Pictures took over the lease of the La Scala building and renamed it The Capitol. It showed the first 'talking film' in Ireland, *The Singing Fool*, on 21 April 1929, which starred Al Jolson (1886–1950), in blackface, as a waiter who goes on to become a Broadway star.

In *Cinema and Ireland*, Kevin Rockett writes about the 1 July 1929 screening of the first Irish sound film that was also shown in the Capitol. It was the Catholic Emancipation Centenary celebrations and, presumably, plenty of nuns and priests forked out the price of a ticket and took their seat, only to discover that the programme also included two Hollywood comedies and a performance by the dance group the Twelve Capitol Tiller Girls.

Films were shown on a loop as a general practice, meaning that customers could take their seats midway through a screening, obliging them to remain for the next show in order to catch what they had missed. Accordingly, the Capitol's first show of the day started at 2.45pm and the same film continued to play, every half-hour, until 11pm. Sundays were different with only two screenings available, at 3pm and 8pm.

The Capitol supplemented its schedule with a weekly live show, providing a stage and audience for the likes of Margaret Tisdall (1906–79) who was better known as Peggy Dell, the Irish singer and pianist.

It shared the Metropole's fate, closing in 1972 and being pulled down to make way for the new British Home Stores.

THE AMBASSADOR

The Ambassador has a particularly long history, stemming from its 1764 début as the Rotunda's Round Room. It was a popular spot for social events. In her diaries, published as *Retrospections of Dorothea Herbert 1770–1806*, Dorothea describes a party that she attends with her aunt and sister in 1779, referring to it specifically as a 'Rotunda Party'. Decked out to the nines, her family group enjoyed their evening until Aunt Herbert unwittingly caused them much embarrassment when she mistook another woman for her own daughter and walked the room, leaning on her arm. A minor offence, surely, only that the aunt was leaning on the arm of one Catherine Netterville, a famous prostitute, who was known professionally as Kitty Cut-A-Dash, and happened to be wearing the same white lutestring silk dress as Aunt Herbert's daughter Fanny. Following this mishap, the Herberts stayed home awhile, before braving society once more. This Catherine Netterville may or may not be Lady Catherine Netterville whose granddaughter was abducted from her Sackville House in 1775.

In June 1855, another Rotunda party features in the diary of Elizabeth

The Ambassador was once the Rotunda's Round Room.

Grant of Rothiemurchus. It is a Cavalry Ball and, therefore, distinctly military in theme. She describes a troop of Dragoons in position around the Rotunda, every second soldier bearing a torch. Three large guns were decorated with torches and more soldiers were positioned at the doorway, their helmets shining like gold beneath the flames of even more torches. Inside, guests walked the long passage, which was lined with soldiers, to the door of the Round Room, where one was officially greeted by the committee. Flags of all kinds adorned the walls, and there were plenty of flowers. Inside the brightly lit Pillar Room, where music was being played, there were neither guns nor flags, only flowers. It seems that all the rooms were used; the Long Room posed as the drawing room, and the smaller Long Room was where the food was being served. The diarist records that the table was laid out with great generosity and in perfect taste.

From 1897 onwards, the Rotunda showed the occasional film until 1910, when a commitment was made and it began showing films full time for a maximum capacity of 736 customers. This was where Charlie Chaplin first appeared on screen in Dublin, in the 1914 comedy *Making a Living*.

Nicknamed 'The Roxy' or 'The Roto', the cinema was taken over by Capital and Allied Theatres Ltd in the 1940s and proved a sound investment. By the 1950s, there was money to extend it, enlarging its seating capacity to 1,200, including 500 in a new balcony, along with private boxes. It also changed its name to the Ambassador. The opening night on 23 September 1954 was a gala performance in itself, with the new cinema being launched by Dublin's lord mayor, Alfie Byrne (1882–1956).

A highlight in its history was the 1966 screening of the war film *The Blue Max*. Starring George Peppard (1928–94), James Mason (1909–84) and Ursula Andress (*b.* 1936), it tells the story of a German fighter pilot in the First World War. Made in Ardmore Studios in Bray, County Wicklow, Dublin landmarks Christ Church Cathedral and Leinster House were filmed to represent Berlin. Twentieth Century Fox had nine war planes built for $250,000 and one of them graced the Ambassador on the film's opening night.

Ten years later, in 1977, the cinema closed temporarily before re-opening under a new owner, the Green Group, who ran it for the next decade, during which it showed mostly children's films until it closed once more. Another new owner made an entrance, the cinema chain Ward Anderson, who did their best to maintain it and received a boost in 1997 thanks to the James Cameron (*b*. 1954) epic *Titanic*. However, the lows literally outnumbered the highs. For instance, when the cinema ran the re-issue of the 1935 film *The Informer*, set during the Irish War of Independence, some of the screenings involved an audience of two. Running a single screen became an impossibility in the age of the multiplexes and the Ambassador eventually shut its doors in 1999. Yet, all was not lost. MCD Productions, the entertainment promotors, leased the building until 2008, transforming it into a venue for concerts for the likes of Vampire Weekend and Wyclef Jean. In 2007, there was talk of turning the building into Dublin's new city library, but those plans were shelved in 2011 because the building was deemed too small. It is still in use today as an event and exhibition venue.

James Gandon (1743–1823), the English architect who designed Carlisle Bridge.

CHAPTER FIVE

O'Connell Street
Bridge

J ust like the street, O'Connell Bridge was a later incarnation of an initial construction.

Today, it seems an obvious location for a bridge. Back in 1761, a sixteen-page pamphlet entitled 'Reasons for a new Bridge' was published to counter an article in *Faulkner's Journal* that protested the idea of a bridge in an area of little importance in comparison to the area surrounding Essex Bridge (Grattan Bridge) which was judged to be the city's central point. The argument continued for twenty years, finally ending in 1782 with Parliament giving its blessing for the Wide Streets Commissioners to proceed with bridging the north and south banks of the River Liffey to the east of Essex Bridge. Furthermore, they approved two avenues stemming from the new bridge, the first leading to the House of Lords, in College Green, while the second would lead to Townsend Street and the east of Dublin. Those new avenues were named Westmoreland Street after John Fane, 10th Earl of Westmoreland (1759–1841) and D'Olier Street after Jeremiah D'Olier (1754–1817), a goldsmith and City Sheriff in 1788 and one of the first to live in Mountjoy Square.

In the 1909 Christmas edition of *The Lady of the House*, which claimed to be Ireland's first magazine for women, the article 'The Street Life of Old Dublin' discusses the impact of the bridge and Sackville Street on Dublin, suggesting that they altered the entire flow of the city's traffic. It also queried the need for Carlisle Bridge. According to the article, the need for another bridge arose once Gandon's Beresford Bridge was completed at Custom House in 1791, highlighting the fact that the nearest other bridge was over a mile away, which could 'not be endured' by the Wide Streets Commission. The article applauds the MP, the Right Honourable John Beresford (1738–1805), in particular, declaring that any cultured Irish person must appreciate how they have benefited from his 'long nursed' vision, which resulted in the building of Custom House and the complete transformation of the surrounding area.

Beresford was good friends with Chief Secretary William Eden (1745–1814), who had written to him in 1782 to request that:

If our great plans should ever go into execution for the improvement of Dublin, I beg that you will contrive to edge my name into some street or into some square, opening to a bridge, the bank or the Four Courts.

Eden's wish was granted in 1796, long after he had returned to England, when Beresford named the thoroughfare leading to Sackville Street and the new bridge Eden Place, thereby cementing this friendship, which proved beneficial when a new Lord Lieutenant, William Wentworth Fitzwilliam (1748–1833), was appointed in August 1794.

He was the 4th Earl Fitzwilliam and one of the richest men in Britain, and he arrived in Ireland the following January, to take up his new position and promptly fired Beresford from his Commissioner of Customs post. Beresford responded by writing to William Eden, who made such a fuss that Fitzwilliam was recalled three months later. However, the magazine doesn't mention that Fitzwilliam believed in equal rights for Catholics. After accepting the job, he had written to his friend Henry Grattan (1746–1820) to declare:

> I shall not do my duty if I do not distinctly state as my opinion that not to grant cheerfully on the part of government all the Catholics wish will not only be exceedingly impolitic but perhaps dangerous …

This was not a popular attitude for Beresford and his peers in Dublin.

Carlisle Bridge was the first bridge to be constructed downstream from the Essex area and the lowest bridge over the River Liffey for some time. It replaced a ferry and was built by English architect James Gandon (1743–1823), opening to pedestrians in 1794 and named after the then lord lieutenant of Ireland, Frederick Howard, the 5th Earl of Carlisle (1748–1825).

Six years later, the bridge was put to dire use on 14 June when Wexford man Doctor John Esmonde (c. 1760–98) was hung from its scaffolding, his yeoman coat turned inside out to show off his treachery. A Catholic, the doctor had settled in Kildare in 1785, where he married Helen Callan, a wealthy heiress. There were always two sides to his coat, if you like, in that as a paid-up member of Kildare's gentry, he campaigned for more help and relief for poor Catholics. In 1796, he was made first lieutenant to Richard Griffith (1752–1820) of Clane's yeomanry calvary corps. Two years later, he joined Kildare's United Irishmen and was made treasurer. Inspired by events happening across Europe, the United Irishmen wanted to reform Ireland's parliamentary system and end discrimination of Irish Catholics. Following a meeting on the evening of 23 May, at Doctor Esmonde's house, to finalise plans for a United Irishmen rebellion, an attack was made on the barracks at Prosperous that resulted in the deaths of several members of North Cork's militia. Esmonde's name was leaked as the leader of this attack by yeoman Mite who told Richard Griffith that he had accompanied Esmonde to Prosperous but disappeared as soon as the fighting started. Naively believing that he could maintain his association with his fellow yeomen whilst fighting for Ireland's freedom with the 'rebels', Esmonde turned up to lead the troops, his hair combed and boots polished, and found himself placed under arrest by his own captain, Richard Griffith, who sent him to Dublin where he was put on trial and condemned to death.

Gandon's original design for the bridge was rather flamboyant, involving one huge arch, sandwiched by colonnade walkways and bearing a massive equestrian statue of King George III (1738–1820). Deemed too expensive, Gandon was obliged to submit something less costly, involving three smaller arches supporting a humpbacked bridge, made from Portland stone and granite. A walk across this bridge was punctuated by a group of obelisks (tall, narrow stone) which would have reminded the well-travelled of similar sights in the likes of Venice and Paris.

Decorative keystones on the arches were to be provided by Meath man Edward Smyth (1749–1812), who had sculpted his interpretation of Anna Livia (Liffey) and the Atlantic Ocean.

Smyth was well known for his river head keystones on the Custom House. His father was either a sea captain or a stone cutter and the family settled in Dublin in 1850. Smyth attended the Dublin Society Art School, which was established in 1749. Initially, the school only offered lessons in drawing until 1811, when thanks to its sponsors it could afford to provide lessons in modelling and sculpture. A definite turning point in Smyth's career was his being apprenticed to Londoner sculptor Simon Vierpyl (c. 1725–1810) in the mid to late 1770s. Vierpyl had spent nine years in Rome copying original statues for wealthy tourists, such as Irish statesman

James Caulfield (1728–99). A committed fan and patron, the viscount gave Vierpyl his biggest commission ever when he asked for terracotta copies of twenty-two statues and seventy-eight busts from Rome's Capitoline Museum. He also changed the course of Vierpyl's life by inviting him to come to Ireland. Vierpyl packed up his Italian home in October 1756, arriving in Ireland before the end of the year.

Perhaps he wanted a break from sculpting. In Ireland, Vierpyl expanded his interests by getting involved with various building projects as a stone carver or mason, including a brief stint on the 'orchestra' in the Rotunda Gardens. During the late 1770s, he supervised work on the Poolbeg Lighthouse. Dublin Corporation employed him as a craftsman throughout the 1780s. Meanwhile, he also discovered a passion for real estate. He bought and developed seven separate plots of land, from Parnell Square to the North Wall.

Vierpyl's story became entwined with Sackville Street's in 1784 after his house and surrounding property in Bachelor's Walk were procured by the Wide Streets Commission in order to extend the street to the river. His cooperation netted him £2,374 in compensation.

Unfortunately, Edward Smyth's heads were too big for the new arches and so 'inferior', according to Christine Casey, copies were made by sculptor Charles William Harrison (1834–1903). Smyth's original heads ended up decorating the Tropical Fruit Warehouse on Sir John Rogerson's Quay, where they remain today, supervising the warehouse's redevelopment into what a spokesman from the Dublin Civic Trust describes as a Grade A office space, complete with glazed floors that will float over the building.

The Dublin-based Brocas family shared at least one particular talent as throughout the late mid-eighteenth and early nineteenth century they produced five artists over two generations, headed by father Henry (c. 1762–1837), a self-taught artist, and his four sons: James Henry (1790–1846), Samuel Frederick (1792–1847), William (c. 1794–1868) and Henry (*c.* 1798–1873). Between them, they provided approximately 2,500 pictures and etchings and, amongst other subjects, twelve views of Dublin between 1818 and 1829.

We can step back to 1820 and view Westmoreland Street from Carlisle Bridge thanks to Samuel capturing it in coloured pencil and Henry following up with an etching.

The sky is clear and perhaps it is the weekend, a Saturday afternoon, as it appears that the middle class are free to take their constitutional. The men are in morning coats and top hats whilst the ladies wear flouncy dresses and are protected from the sun by wide-brimmed bonnets and parasols. A young husband and wife are hand in hand with their little daughter who is dressed like her mother. There are no beggars or urchins in sight and, apart from the drivers of the horse carriages in the background, the only working-class person depicted is that of the street hawker Treacle Billie, in a top hat and coat, selling his doughnuts filled with treacle.

Henry Brocas's etching of Carlisle Bridge, today's O'Connell Bridge, in 1810.

Engineer and keen astronomer Binden Blood Stoney rebuilt Carlisle Bridge in 1877.

In 2019, Adams Fine Arts and Auctioneers put a 'Trade Card of Law' up for sale with a maximum estimated price tag of €300. The card, which promoted Mr Law's goldsmith jewellery and watchmaker shop at number 1 Sackville Street, is adorned with a Georgian landscape of Dublin and includes a detailed view of Carlisle Bridge with its two-headed oil lamps and obelisks companions. Just beyond the bridge are several ships masts and the Custom House just beyond that again. The card was sold for €600.

By 1860, Gandon's bridge was in dire need of a salvage job as it was too narrow for nineteenth-century Dublin and the progressive upsurge in her traffic and population. In fact, in 1852, it was identified as the most dangerous bridge in the British Empire due to its increasingly unstable foundations, and only just performed its basic duty with the assistance of the baton-wielding policemen who forced pedestrians and horses to keep moving over it for fear of a complete blockage.

In 1872, the city elders held a competition to improve the situation. Once again, the bridge was the subject of much debate, this time between Dublin Corporation and the Dublin Port and Docks Board. It took another four years before the right man volunteered for the job. Binden Blood Stoney (1828–1909) was chief engineer to the Dublin Port and Docks Board. Born in County Offaly, he moved to Dublin with his mother and siblings following his father's death, where he studied at Trinity College's School of Engineering, graduating in 1850 with a diploma in Civil Engineering. His first job required him to move back to his native county after he was hired as assistant astronomer to William Parsons, the 3rd Earl of Rosse (1800–67). Parsons built the 72-inch (182-centimetre) 'Leviathan', the biggest telescope of the nineteenth century, on the grounds of Birr Castle. Stoney used it to correctly map the spiral form of the Andromeda Galaxy, the huge collection of stars, dust and gas that make up the nearest major galaxy to the Milky Way and is 2.5 million light years from earth – and, incidentally, is due to collide with the Milky Way in approximately 4.5 billion years from now.

Stoney's first proper engineering position was as resident engineer on the Boyne Viaduct. His entry in the *Dictionary of Irish Architects* does not mention his all-important rebuild of Carlisle Bridge in 1877, whereby he widened the bridge thrice over to correspond with the width of Sackville Street and also flattened out the steep curve of Gandon's bridge. Actually, this was just one project out of a remit that saw him redesign and rebuild

The Earl of Rosse owned the 'Leviathan', the biggest telescope of the nineteenth century, which still stands today on the grounds of Birr Castle in County Offaly.

LORD ROSS'S TELESCOPE. BIRR. 3237. W.L.

7,000 feet of quay walls on the north and south banks of the Liffey, as well as Grattan Bridge and Beresford Bridge at Custom House.

Stoney's new and improved Carlisle Bridge, whose width had been increased to 230 feet (70 metres) reopened in 1880. Dublin Corporation wanted to rename it as O'Connell Bridge and did not hide their disdain for its existing name, actually covering up the red marble plaque engraved with 'Carlisle Bridge' with a bronze-green plaque that read, '[this plaque] which greets the passer-by today who little dreams that the brilliance of Dan envelopes the dullness of the Earl.' Two years later, the bridge was finally rechristened as O'Connell Bridge.

By 1929, the bridge would once more prove a source of frustration to Dubliners and the cry went out for new bridges across the Liffey. Writing in *The Irish Times* about the city centre's traffic congestion, the President of the Institute of Civil Engineers, Alfred Delap (1871–1943), lamented how O'Connell Bridge was being wasted as a resource as roughly half of it was being used as a carpark, not to mention the two sets of tram tracks either side of the parked cars. Looking at photographs taken in the mid to late 1920s, it is obvious that all manner of vehicles shared the space allotted to the tram tracks, in that the traffic jams on the bridge were awash with trams, cars, lorries and motorbikes.

Mr Delap believed in improving upon the bridges already in place before looking to build more. Accordingly, measures were taken to promote easier movement around the bridge and O'Connell Street. In 1929, the statue of William O'Brien was moved from the busy intersection of D'Olier and Westmoreland Streets to O'Connell Street. Dublin Corporation wanted to relocate Nelson's Pillar as they considered it an obstacle to free-flowing traffic. As late as 1938, at a meeting of the Royal Irish Automobile Club, consideration was given to the somewhat shocking suggestion that Daniel O'Connell's monument be moved away from O'Connell Street as a further possible solution to traffic congestion.

An early twentieth-century photograph showing how cars parked on O'Connell Bridge.

When it was finally determined to implement the necessary, and costly, changes to the bridge, the question arose as to who might foot the bill. It was generally agreed that the work should revolve around the tram tracks, that is, remove the two inner sets, while the outer one on the west side of the bridge would be given over to the north-bound city trams and the east side would belong to the south-going tram. This meant extra expense and labour to enable trams to change direction and those expecting the Dublin United Tramway Company to open its wallet were to be disappointed. Similarly, the Ports and Docks Board would not be providing funds as it was concentrating its interest on Butt Bridge. So, it was left to Dublin Corporation to pay for the restyling of O'Connell Bridge with a government grant that was not large enough to cover all the desired changes. As usual, with this bridge, a compromise on the initial vision was financially necessary.

O'Connell Bridge was central to an extraordinary occasion when it hosted the final address of the 1932 Eucharistic Congress. This was arguably Ireland's first opportunity to show off her capital city via a majestic event that seemed expressly designed for this newly independent and predominantly Catholic country, while also providing a crowning moment that had nothing to do with England's royals and countrymen. Hosting the Eucharistic Congress brought numerous benefits that were played out in political, historical and economical terms.

The organising of such an event was such a mammoth task that a country was given several years to prepare. Accordingly, The Permanent Committee of the International Eucharistic Congresses announced Dublin as the 1932 location back in December 1929. Throughout 1930, *The Irish Times* printed a series of articles expressing the need for accommodation, an extra 8,000 beds all told, and more restaurants and cafés to cope with a million visitors, national and international. The College of Surgeons was to be transformed into an upmarket restaurant, while University College

A crowning moment for Dublin, the 1932 Eucharistic Congress.

Dublin's cafeteria, in Belfield, would be opened to the public. However, even before new restaurants could be established, the paper reported that the cookery classes were being put on in a technical institute in order to have enough cooks.

The work paid off and Dublin's beauty was appreciated by the likes of GK (Gilbert Keith) Chesterton (1874–1936), the English writer, journalist and critic, who gave an account of the week-long congress in his book *Christendom in Dublin*. He paid Dublin many compliments, observing how even the tenements, decked out in flowers and flags, and Dublin's poor had been included in the festivities. He also quotes an old woman who was worrying that weather might turn and ruin everything before concluding, 'Well, if it rains now, He'll have brought it on Himself!'

On Sunday, 26 June, it is estimated that a million people attended mass in the Phoenix Park and then made their way on foot to O'Connell Street and Bridge. This procession, described as 'miles of praying people', was heading for the 5.30pm service of Benediction and hymns in which the Cardinal Lorenzo Lauri (1864–1941) as Papal Legate, the Pope's Representative, would give his final address. Six days earlier, he sailed into Dún

Laoghaire on SS *Cambria*, to be met by huge ecstatic crowds that included 36,000 school children, who cheered as the Irish air force flew overhead in the formation of a crucifix.

Guiney's newly enlarged shop on Talbot Street did a roaring trade in white frocks and suits to be worn at the outdoor masses and ceremonies, whilst around the corner, Clery's struggled to sell off its enormous stock of similar items at presumably superior prices.

The photographs of the final address are quite dramatic. The statue of Daniel O'Connell, the great Liberator of 1829, stands tall in the midst of thousands of Catholics on their knees who were reaping the benefits of his efforts 103 years earlier.

Apart from the Eucharistic Congress, 1932 was a pivotal year in Irish history as the general election would be the first to take place since the Statute of Westminster granted full independence to the Irish Free State in 1931. There was a great deal of nervousness attached to this election. If outvoted, would the reigning Cumann na nGaedheal, popular with the Catholic Church, leave quietly? After all, the opposing parties Fianna Fáil and the Labour Party included men who would have been sworn enemies during the Civil War.

WT Cosgrave, who had been President since 1922, brought the election forward to February so that it would be done and dusted by the time the cardinal arrived in June. Fianna Fáil's ensuing triumph at the polls meant that the new president, Éamon de Valera, who had been excommunicated from the church for his anti-Treaty stance, was the one to welcome the cardinal to Ireland.

Reflecting on his visit, Cardinal Lauri remembers standing on the ship and waving at the huge crowd. He could see the diplomatic corps and bishops on the pier, but for some moments he and his companions were stricken by the fact that there seemed to be no government officials in sight, hardly daring to think what that might mean. Just then, a group of men in

Cardinal Lorenzo Lauri onstage at O'Connell Bridge. President Éamon de Valera can be seen left of the cardinal.

dark coats and soft hats made their approach and introduced themselves as the President of Ireland and his ministers. The visitors had assumed them to be detectives. An *Irish Times* reporter criticised the President's 'sartorial politics' in his article on 21 June 1932, as neither de Valera nor his council were in full morning dress, unlike the members of the Congress Reception Committee and the Dún Laoghaire Borough Council.

In any case, despite his complex relationship with the clergy, de Valera was a committed Catholic who was more than happy to play a prominent role that week, which could only improve his popularity amongst a nation of stalwart churchgoers. Irish Protestants, Jews and so on must have felt disconnected by this unprecedented outpouring of nationalism in its purest form, a united fervour for all things Irish and Roman. In fact, one business saw an opportunity to capitalise on the atmosphere. In the *Advance Programme to the Eucharistic Congress (1932)*, O'Hanrahan's gramophone shop, which was next door to Findlater's, placed an advertisement in the pamphlet, urging people to shop at Catholic businesses only and, thereby, not fund 'anti-Catholics'.

Moreover, the President would prove where his allegiances lay when he introduced Ireland's new constitution in 1937, a sacred document that so obviously adhered to a singular Catholic ethos in terms of the Irish citizen's private and domestic life,.

In 1949, the final constitutional tie to England was dissolved as twenty-six counties in Ireland left the British Commonwealth and finally became a republic. On Sunday night, 17 April, thousands of men, women and children took up positions on O'Connell Street Bridge and Street in order to see in the new dawn on Easter Monday, the first day of Ireland's independence proper. A salute of twenty-one guns was fired at midnight, or just after, as it had proved difficult for the riflemen to get into place, such was the amount of people on the bridge. After the shots rang out, the national anthem was played, and one may assume plenty of tears were shed as there surely was much reflection about the sacrifices made by thousands of Irishmen and women along the way.

In April 2020, the Dublin Civic Trust wrote about Gandon's Carlisle Bridge on their popular Facebook page. Incredibly, the original 1790s' balustrades are still in existence today and form an attractive boundary for the garden at Clonturk House, a religious institution in Drumcondra that underwent refurbishment in 1880.

Witnesses described an angry police force beating up unarmed civilians following their arrest of James Larkin in August 1913.

CHAPTER SIX

Murder and Mayhem on O'Connell Street

AUGUST 1854

Ahorrific double murder took place in August 1854. A retired rural doctor and his wife arrived to stay at the Imperial Hotel in order to visit its immediate neighbour, the new 'monster store', the Palatial Mart, Clery's predecessor.

Costello and Farmer, in their book *The Very Heart of the City: The Story of Denis Guiney & Clerys*, describe what happened next. The elderly couple befriended the head porter and accepted his kind offer to show them around Dublin. He must have gained their trust as they agreed to place their cash, a box of gold coins, in his care. It is not known how honourable his intentions were initially, but in any case, he and a friend broke open the box and gambled away its contents. In desperation, the porter filled the box with coppers but when the doctor asked for its return, the porter must have panicked and took the next dastardly step. He lured the couple into a quiet part of the building where his accomplice lay in wait and between them,

201

they strangled the doctor and his wife.

The story does not end there. Over 132 years later, in June 1986, a sales assistant went into the storeroom that was behind the Roland Cartier stand. As the shop was closed, she was surprised to find an elderly woman there, dressed in dark, unfashionable clothes. On informing the 'customer' that the shop was closed, the lady vanished before her eyes.

That same year, members of the ITGWU (Irish Transport and General Workers' Union) refused to go into a storeroom after one of them saw a ghostly figure go in first. Meanwhile, other staff claimed to see an elderly gentleman meandering around the store after hours, whilst security guards reported hearing footsteps at night.

It is tempting to imagine that the storeroom might just have been the 1854 crime scene.

SUNDAY, 31 AUGUST 1913

The writer and historian RF Foster describes the 1913 Lockout as a failure because it never brought any essential industry to a halt as a large number of non-union workers were made available. Where it did succeed, however, was in cementing the concept of harnessing workers together in order to implement change, and this was thanks to James Connolly and the Liverpool-born trade unionist James Larkin. And, surely, one also has to take into consideration Larkin's nemesis, Corkonian and business magnate William Martin Murphy.

That August, tensions were rising between the police and workers due to the Irish Transport and General Workers' Union calling on Tram drivers to come out on strike on Tuesday, 26 August, nine days after 200 drivers lost their jobs, owing to mere suspicion that they were involved with the ITGWU.

The Dublin United Tramway Company was just one of the businesses owned by William Martin Murphy, who went to Dublin Castle to request more help from the Dublin Metropolitan Police (DMP). A former (anti-Parnellite) politician, Murphy had bought out the bankrupt *Irish Daily Independent* newspaper in 1900, relaunching it as the *Irish Independent*; six years later, he created its sibling, the *Sunday Independent*.

The tram drivers had been told to disembark their trams near Nelson's Pillar at 9.40am. Within hours, Murphy had brought in scab workers (strike breakers) who took over the abandoned trams.

A heavily advertised protest was organised for Sunday, 31 August, but following violent clashes on Tuesday after scab drivers arrived to replace the strikers, James Larkin and his fellow trade union officials were arrested in their homes on 28 August and jailed in Mountjoy. Meanwhile, a magistrate named EG Swifte, who owned shares in Murphy's tramway company and was known for his harsh sentences, issued a proclamation forbidding Sunday's protest from taking place. Lines were quickly being drawn by Larkin. Upon his release from Mountjoy, he headed for Liberty Hall where, from a window, he set fire to the judge's proclamation and swore to be in Sackville Street on Sunday, 'dead or alive'.

Spending the night of Saturday, 30 August in hiding in Countess Markievicz's (1868–1927) house, Larkin received a 'makeover' from Markievicz's friend and fellow activist Helena Molony (1883–1967), an Abbey theatre actress who had joined the Irish Citizen Army (ICA). It was imperative to get Larkin to his destination – Murphy's Metropole Hotel on Sackville Street – without his being recognised by the police. In fact, Larkin's colleagues saw fit to

Helena Molony.

James Larkin in disguise after his arrest at the Imperial Hotel in Dublin.

move the protest to Croydon Park in Fairview. Larkin, however, intended to make good on his word to speak at the original location. So, he was dressed up to look like a seventy-year-old clergyman. Neither Markievicz nor Molony could accompany him as they were known to the police, who were on standby in clusters in and around Sackville Street.

In fact, officers had been confined to their barracks that weekend and ordered to remain in full uniform. Therefore, Markievicz's young friend Nellie Gifford (1880–1971), sister of Grace – the future wife of Joseph Plunkett, one of the executive leaders of the Rising – went with Larkin in a cab that left them at the door of the hotel, where two rooms had been booked for a Mr Donnelly (Larkin) and his niece. They went in and headed up the stairs where Larkin made for the balcony overlooking the street and shouted, 'I'm Larkin!' He managed no more than a few sentences before police rushed into the hotel and arrested him once more.

What happened next perhaps garnered the movement more support and sympathy than any speech Larkin could have made that day. The police, hyped up from a week of violent clashes – and even drunk, according to some eyewitnesses – unleashed their batons on anyone who was walking along Sackville Street. And the street was busy with people, oblivious to Larkin's mission, out for a Sunday stroll and a spot of window shopping. Some of the people left bleeding on the street had no connections with the ITGWU but were simply on the wrong street at the wrong time. According to an eyewitness, the beatings continued for an hour or so.

Then the numbers poured in with *The Daily Sketch* reporting two deaths, 460 injured and 210 arrests, while *The Saturday Post* claimed that 600 injured citizens needed hospital care, including young children and elderly citizens. Newspaper photographs showing the police in action shocked not just Irish citizens but British too. It was a forerunner of what happened three years later when brute force converted generations of hearts and minds to supporting the warriors and martyrs of 1916.

MONDAY, 24 APRIL 1916

In his memoir, Desmond Fitzgerald (1888–1947), Ireland's future Minister of Defence and father of future Taoiseach, Garret, describes his visit to the GPO after it had been taken over by the rebels. As he was greeted by friends, two Swedish men popped into the post office to ask if they could join in the fighting as they disliked the English. Their only stipend being that they would have to leave early on Thursday to get their boat home.

Everyone was smiling, including his old friend The O'Rahilly (Michael Joseph O'Rahilly, 1875–1916), who showed Desmond around. He asked The O'Rahilly, who initially had been against the Rising, how long he thought they could hold out. Less than twenty-four hours was the reply which Desmond thought was wildly optimistic. He was shown the large restaurant and noted the huge quantity of food available. Desmond also saw four young privates who had been taken prisoner. They were eager to help the rebels and show off their extensive knowledge of the building. Meanwhile, a captured lieutenant, who just happened to be in the GPO when it was taken over, looked miserable as he supped from a bottle of brandy.

After the tour, Desmond and The O'Rahilly both confessed their belief that they would all be wiped out within a matter of hours. They also agreed that The O'Rahilly had been treated badly by the others who had left him out of their plans while he was busy spreading the word that the Rising was postponed. Desmond had to report to Pádraig Pearse, Tom Clarke and James Connolly. Pearse was the only one who admitted regret at what had happened with The O'Rahilly. Clarke was still smarting about the countermanding order to hold off, but told Fitzgerald that he admired The O'Rahilly more than any other man, while Connolly looked too angry to chat.

Fitzgerald describes meeting another prisoner, the policeman who had been stationed in the Post Office and was now sitting on a chair, nursing

The O'Rahilly was shot twice as he led his men to safety from a burning GPO.

a bottle of Guinness. Someone had taken his boots, allowing Fitzgerald to judge the poor state of his woolly grey socks, which were matted with holes. Feeling sorry for him, Fitzgerald spoke to the policeman and was surprised to hear him lamenting that his being taken hostage might cost him his job. Fitzgerald felt the prisoner's situation was far more serious, in that he might well share the fate that Fitzgerald believed would ultimately befall the rebels – that of death.

The standoff in the GPO lasted longer than expected. Instead of hours, Pearse and his men held out for days until Friday brought the devastation that Fitzgerald and his old friend had expected.

By Friday, Sackville Street and the GPO were in flames and, by Friday night, The O'Rahilly's sacrifice for his country was complete. He had disagreed with the timing of the Rebellion, but on discovering that it was going ahead, presented himself to Pearse and Connolly and followed orders that he fully expected to be the death of him. He had volunteered to lead a party of men from the burning GPO, reaching Moore Street before a few of them, including himself, were shot. Somehow, he managed to get himself to Sackville Lane before being shot again. He lay dying and an elderly woman heard his cry for water. Several times, glass in hand, she tried to reach him but was kept back by British snipers at the nearby barricade. Finally, she went out to him but tripped in the dark, spilling the water. This was the last straw for her and she screamed at the soldiers, 'May God forgive you that you wouldn't let me give a drink to a dying man!'

SUNDAY, 21 NOVEMBER 1920

One of the most tragic days in Irish history began with two killings in the Gresham Hotel. Just before 9am, nine Irishmen made the short walk from Parnell Square to the Gresham on a mission for their boss, Michael Collins.

Initially, a list of fifty names had been compiled until Ireland's Minister for Defence Cathal Brugha's (1874–1922) protests forced Collins to shorten his list. That Sunday morning, the targets were British men who were believed to be members of the Cairo Gang, a group of British intelligence officers who had been brought to Ireland to investigate and probably assassinate the leaders of the Irish Republican Army. The name of the group may have come from the location for many of their meetings, the Cairo Café on Grafton Street.

Collins's handpicked soldiers were only given their orders on Saturday night. For the most part, the men were young, including seventeen-year-old Charlie Dalton (brother of Emmet), and the names on the list would have meant nothing to them. Sleep was hard to come by for young men who had never killed before.

The Gresham Hotel was one of several hotels and guest houses to be hit the following morning but was the only one targeted on the northside of the city. Historian Donal Fallon, writing on the hundredth anniversary of the shootings, points out that questions remain about what happened that morning in the Gresham – that is, who exactly was killed.

James Cahill, a young man from Cavan, was attached to D Company of the Second Battalion of the Dublin Brigade. He and his eight colleagues had been delegated to kill three British intelligence officers who were staying in the hotel. Their party was to split the killings three ways, with Cahill, Nick Leonard and Mick Kelly doing the shootings, whilst the other six dealt with hotel staff and residents.

As they approached the Gresham's front door, Cahill heard a newsboy call out his name in greeting. However, a second newsboy immediately hushed the first with the words, 'There's a job on. Best to clear out!'

Once inside, they cut the phones and, after checking the registrar book, forced head porter Hugh Callaghan to lead them first to Room 14, which housed Lieutenant Leonard Wilde. Seeing a man in the corridor, they asked him to identify himself. On receiving the reply, 'Alan Wilde, British Intelligence Officer. Just back from Spain', Kelly shot him dead. Wilde must have thought they were policemen.

Then they made their way upstairs to Room 24, where they found ex-Captain Patrick McCormack in bed, reading his newspaper. James Cahill said that McCormack had his .38 revolver in his hand and fired it at the intruders. Without a word, Cahill and Kelly poured five bullets into him at point-blank range; the blood splattered right across the room.

Their third target was not in his room, and moments later, Cahill and his colleagues were back out on O'Connell Street.

Afterwards, there was great controversy over the identity of the two

National Army soldiers approach the Gresham Hotel, which was occupied by the IRA during the fighting.

men, with English newspapers protesting their innocence. Meanwhile, Archbishop Patrick Clune (1864–1935) reassured the Gresham's manager James Doyle that Wilde, at least, was indeed a British spy and therefore deserving of his fate. However, Donal Fallon relates how three days earlier, Wilde had written to Arthur Henderson of the British Labour Party about the Irish situation, adding that 'Ireland is essentially a tradition-loving people and her traditions must be respected by those who govern her.' Fallon wonders if the misguided Wilde was in Dublin on his own mission to help the people of Ireland.

The Archbishop's nephew Conor also died that same day in mysterious circumstances in Dublin Castle.

Patrick McCormack, on the other hand, had been a veterinary surgeon with the British Army and was only in Ireland to buy race horses for the Alexandria Turf Club before returning to his wife and children in Egypt. Afterwards, Michael Collins agreed that McCormack's death had been a

An anti-Treaty rally on O'Connell Street in early 1922; the speakers standing by the tricolour are not known.

mistake. A Catholic, McCormack was buried at Glasnevin Cemetery.

A lot more died that Sunday afternoon when hell was unleashed in Croke Park by British forces out for revenge.

WEDNESDAY, 5 JULY 1922

Described by Emmet Dalton as a 'lovable fanatic', Cathal Brugha began the year by voting against the Anglo-Irish Treaty while accidentally scoring some votes for the Treaty after criticising Michael Collins for being nothing more than a 'middleman', perhaps irked by Arthur Griffith's claim that Collins was the man who had won the War of Independence. Collins's popularity was a sore point for him.

Before the first shot of the Civil War was fired, Brugha had begged his anti-Treaty colleagues not to fight their fellow Irishmen. When the IRA took over the Four Courts, Brugha and Oscar Traynor, republican and future Minister for Defence, asked them to leave and when they wouldn't, Traynor stationed troops on and around O'Connell Street in an attempt to distract attention from the Four Courts, which might then allow space for negotiations to be initiated.

By July, the 'Battle for Dublin' had moved to the hotels on O'Connell

The Hammam Hotel was famous for its Turkish baths.

Street. Brugha, who was in command of the O'Connell Street battalion, was at numbers 11 and 12, in The Hamman Hotel, which was renowned for its Turkish baths.

Seven years after the *Helga* gunboat destroyed most of O'Connell Street, the street was on fire again, only this time the destruction was caused by Irishmen. And, just like the street, the 1916 Rising had almost destroyed Cathal Brugha. During the Easter Rising fighting he had been badly wounded by a hand grenade. His comrades left him where he fell, believing him to be dead, and he was only rescued when Eamonn Ceannt (1881–1916) heard him taunting the British soldiers. However, he was seriously injured, with twenty-five separate wounds – five of which were deemed dangerous and nine serious, including his mangled right leg and hip that resulted in a permanent limp.

Now, in July 1922, Brugha, who bitterly disagreed with the Treaty, was under fire once more. After most of the anti-Treaty forces escaped the fires of O'Connell Street, Brugha remained in place with a small rearguard that included approximately thirty women. Eventually, he ordered his group to leave the hotel and surrender to the Free State troops outside. Three women refused to leave, one of whom was Linda Kearns (1888/9–1951), a nurse and fearless activist who had been jailed in 1920 after being caught driving a car full of IRA guns and ammunition. She saw what happened next. Brugha had ordered his men away to surrender but, for whatever reason, decided against doing it himself. He must have known what might happen when he emerged from the hotel, brandishing his revolver. A shot rang out from Findlater's Place and he fell down, the solitary bullet severing an artery in his left thigh. Linda Kearns ran to him and held the artery between her fingers in the frantic drive to the Mater Hospital. Unfortunately, he had lost too much blood, though the three doctors on duty did their best for him, operating on him within an hour of his arrival. He died two days later at 10.45am, eleven days before his forty-eighth birthday.

FRIDAY, 17 MAY 1974

Three car bombs detonated in Parnell, Talbot and South Leinster Streets that Friday in 1974. This was the third time that The Troubles, (the name given to the Northern Ireland conflict that spanned three decades, from 1968 to 1998) had stretched all the way to Dublin.

On Friday, 1 December 1972, two minutes before 8pm, a blue Hillman Avenger exploded on Eden Quay. Miraculously, no one died, although many were injured. Also, at two minutes before 8pm, the offices of *The Belfast News-Letter* received a phone call from a man with an English accent, who warned that two bombs would explode in Dublin: one at Liberty Hall, while the second would go off on Abbey Street behind Clery's Department Store. The *News-Letter* immediately forwarded the warning to the RUC, who contacted the Garda Control Room at 8.08pm. Officers were dispatched to Sackville Place and Earl Street to clear the area.

There was a CIÉ (Ireland's national public transport provider) staff canteen in Earl Place, and a garda ran in, telling everyone to evacuate the premises. The time was now 8.16pm; the canteen was emptied, and the second bomb, in a silver-grey Ford Escort, exploded on Sackville Place, killing two CIÉ bus conductors who had just left the canteen. Thirty-year-old George Bradshaw and twenty-three year old Thomas Duff were both married with children. Over a hundred people were injured that night.

Thirteen days later, an incendiary device was found in Clery's and two more were found in the Premier Bar on Sackville Place. All had failed to detonate. However, a few weeks later, on Saturday, 20 January 1973, a caller with an English accent rang the telephone exchange on Exchequer Street at 3.08pm with the following warning: 'Listen, love, there is a bomb on O'Connell Street, at the bridge.'

The street would have been busy anyway with weekend shoppers, but because the Irish rugby team were playing the All Blacks at Lansdowne

Road, the city centre was packed with rugby fans and revellers as well as the usual crowds.

At 3.18pm, a man leaving Kilmartin's betting shop on Sackville Place saw smoke pouring out of the boot of a red Vauxhall Victor that was parked outside Egan's pub and faced towards O'Connell Street. Moments later, the car exploded, killing twenty-one-year-old Thomas Douglas, a CIÉ bus conductor – the blast flinging him through a shop window. Fourteen others were seriously injured.

The following year, a Dublin bus strike left the city without public transport for nine weeks over the summer. This was one reason that Talbot Street, in particular, was so busy with pedestrians that Friday, 17 May 1974. It was approaching 5.30pm and people were walking home from work, whilst the shops and cafes were preparing to close their doors.

Within six minutes, Dublin city centre was in disarray and over twenty men, women and children were dead, while some 300 men, women and children suffered a range of injuries. This time, there was no warning phone call. At 5.28pm, a car bomb exploded in Parnell Street; two minutes later a second car bomb exploded in Talbot Street and two minutes after that, a car bomb exploded in South Leinster Street.

At 7pm, a final car bomb exploded in the North Road in County Monaghan, where seven people lost their lives.

On 15 July 1993, the Ulster Volunteer Force claimed they had carried out the Monaghan and Talbot Street bombings. No claims were made about the 1972 and 1973 car bombs. At first the IRA were suspected, but later on it was believed to be the work of one of the Loyalist paramilitary groups. Furthermore, many believed that those who carried out the bombings had been helped by members of the British security forces.

To date, no arrests have been made for any of the bombings.

The St Patrick's Day parade in Dublin hosts marching bands and dancing groups from around the world, as well as local theatrical acts and giant puppets and inflatables, such as this dragon passing by the GPO in 1999.

CHAPTER SEVEN

Gatherings on O'Connell Street

ST PATRICK'S DAY PARADE

In her published diary *Up in the Park*, Elizabeth Shannon (*b.* 1937), wife of the then American ambassador to Ireland, William ('Bill') Shannon (1927–88), describes her excitement at experiencing her first St Patrick's Day in Ireland, in 1978. She devotes an entire entry to that particular 17 March, and it is hard not to nod in agreement as she explains her bitter disappointment. Naturally, the weather features heavily in her account. Every year, the organisers and participants of the St Patrick Day's parade plough ahead with ambition and determination to present the best parade yet, whilst simultaneously praying that the weather will cooperate. Sure enough, as the Shannons took their seats in the reviewing stand on O'Connell Street at 10.30am, the sky was grey, and a cold wind was making itself felt. Not to worry, though, because Bord Fáilte had thoughtfully provided blankets and hot tea for the first-class spectators.

At 11am the Lord Mayor, Michael Collins – the Labour councillor

Left to right: At a reception in the Phoenix Park, Dublin. Sean Donlon, incoming Irish ambassador to the United States of America, Elizabeth McNelly Shannon, Mrs Donlon, Taoiseach Jack Lynch, American Ambassador William V Shannon. Elizabeth Shannon wrote a book about her time in Ireland as the wife of the then American ambassador William Shannon.

who was mayor from 1977 to 1978 – arrived with his wife in a gilded horse-drawn carriage.

Mrs Shannon laments the parade's heavy reliance on rather sombre mobile commercials. For example, one home security firm had several floats in the parade, but instead of paying homage to fun and merriment, they were emblazoned with warnings about the city's growing crime rate to encourage folk to buy their alarms. She describes the hordes of children taking part as 'forlorn'. The youngsters in drum majorette costumes struggling to twirl their batons in the wind were out of step with one another, while their bare arms and legs were blue with the cold.

Next up was a group of elderly American tourists who were doing their best to inject some liveliness into the proceedings. In fact, Mrs Shannon admits to feeling poignant because her compatriots' delight at being part of an Irish St Patrick's Day parade distracted them from the fact that this was not a very good parade at all, and they would have fared better in New York or Boston.

Not surprisingly, her parade highlight was the big brass American army band that had flown in from their base in Germany and succeeded in cheering up an otherwise drab morning. She concludes by reckoning that Ireland needed more practice at putting on parades.

Well, it was true that the Americans – that is, the Irish Americans – were more practised when it came to celebrating St Patrick's Day; they had been marching in his honour since the mid-eighteenth century. Here in Ireland, the day was recognised as a public holiday in 1903 thanks to Irish MP James O'Mara (1873–1948). He introduced the bill in Westminster, where it received the support of many and was duly passed; this was reported by *The Belfast News-Letter* as 'a rare good fortune' for an Irish proposal. Saint Patrick was seen as a man of the people in that he appealed not only to Irish Catholics all across the island, but also to Church of Ireland Protestants, the Welsh and presumably anyone who was not partial to snakes. For instance, the 18 March 1914 edition of the *Northern Whig,* the other popular Belfast page, ran the following:

Irishmen, whatever their creed or politics have an affectionate regard for Saint Patrick's Day and yesterday the shamrock was worn … by nine-tenths of the population of the country.

Of course, following the War of Independence and the Civil War, the Feast Day of Saint Patrick would be imbued with a heightened sense of patriotism.

In any case, Ireland's first parade took place in 1903 in Waterford. Later on, O'Mara found it necessary to introduce a law to ensure that public houses remained closed on 17 March, which was finally overturned in the 1970s.

The official state parade took place in Dublin on 17 March 1931. A minute-long silent video of this first parade can be seen online. If it wasn't captioned as a St Patrick's Day parade, the viewer might be forgiven for thinking that they were watching an army being sent off to war. In fact, this heavily militarised parade was overseen by Ireland's Minister for Defence at the time, Desmond Fitzgerald (1888–1947), father of future Taoiseach, Garret (1926–2011). A handful of dignitaries stand at College Green and salute the Free State's army.

Two years later and the army still dominates the parade in the two minutes of grainy footage online. There is no sound, but one can clearly see how the streets glisten from rainfall, while the guards on duty, in their heavy coats with upturned collars, look perished with the cold.

Future Tánaiste and founding member of Fianna Fáil, Frank Aiken (1898–1983) is Minister for Defence in 1934 and takes the salute. The camera veers away from the usual lines of marching soldiers and armoured cars to show brief, tantalising shots of the ordinary spectators, who look politely interested if not actually excited or entertained.

In 1935, the footage has sound, and as the national army marches along, the camera picks up a mini riot in the background on Dame Street. The British commentator explains that young republicans had been attempting to unfurl black banners. You can see them being baton-charged and chased off by the police.

One of the marching soldiers in the 1938's parade is President de Valera's son, Lieutenant Vivion de Valera (1910–82). The following year, the army are out in force again, this time saluting the first president of Ireland, Douglas Hyde (1860–1949). Possibly the same British commentator, referring to the long process of soldiers, draws attention to the cyclist battalion. Overhead, five planes fly by in formation whilst on the ground the anti-airguns are harmlessly trained on them.

The 1950 parade was more of a celebration, which probably explains why the crowd looks far more relaxed. For one thing, there are no armoured cars nor soldiers in sight. Also, even in the black-and-white film, one can appreciate that the weather was glorious that Friday afternoon. Unlike the previous parades, women and children are involved. In fact, a female piper band leads the procession down O'Connell Street. Behind them are floats advertising Irish produce, including one float bearing the message, 'Don't Force us to emigrate – Buy Irish'. Another float declares that 'Irish Goods Go Best By CIÉ', while a group of grave-looking men in trilby hats and raincoats walk beneath the banner depicting Pádraig Pearse with the words, 'Ireland Still Unfree'.

The men of the old IRA lead the parade down O'Connell Street in 1952. Approximately 75,000 spectators lined both sides of the street to see the 260 vehicles, all representing an aspect of Irishness: from the GAA to the big Guinness trucks, the *Irish Independent* float and Bolands Mills.

Today, the St Patrick's Day festival is the state's biggest annual celebration with the Dublin parade marching its way through the heart of the city; beginning at Parnell Square, it moves down O'Connell Street and over the bridge to Westmoreland Street, turning down Dame Street, then Nicolas Street, Patrick Street and Kevin Street, finally winding up just before St Stephen's Green, at Wexford Street.

In 2019, the festivities in Dublin involved five days of family fun, including a three-day festival village at Merrion Square with a variety of events following the theme of *Scéalaíocht agus Seanchaí* (Stories and Storytellers).

Since 1931, the celebration has only been cancelled twice out of fears for health and safety. In 2001, the parade was cancelled following a nationwide outbreak of foot-and-mouth disease, although tourists and Dubliners

The Irish Independent *photograph that captures an eerily quiet O'Connell Street on 17 March 2020.*

could still toast Saint Patrick in the pub of their choice.

A mere nineteen years later, the unthinkable occurred due to the global Covid-19 pandemic. Following fiery debates, the wise – albeit shocking – decision was made to cancel *everything* in March 2020. There was no parade, no pubs, no parties, no singing throngs clad in fifty shades of green and clutching tiny bunches of shamrocks. Only a couple of shops opened, including the odd mobile stall stacked with Paddy finery, with few potential customers in sight. The *Irish Independent*'s photographer Frank McGrath captured an almost empty O'Connell Street, with a few lone individuals that are almost outnumbered by the socially distancing birds in the foreground.

On 20 January 2021, an announcement was made cancelling the parade for the second year in a row.

CELEBRITY MOTORCADES
1928: *Bremen* Crew

After 'Lucky Lindy' and her pilot, twenty-five-year-old Charles Lindbergh (1902–74), flew direct from New York to Paris in 1927, the question was raised about making the journey in reverse – that is flying direct from Europe to America. It was bound to be more challenging because of prevailing winds and the extra flight time required.

Two determined Germans believed they could do it. The risks were obvious as no less than ten failed attempts to fly East to West had been made in 1927, culminating in the loss of seven lives.

Baron Günther Von Hünefeld (1892–1929) and Captain Hermann Köhl (1888–1938) contacted the Irish government for permission to start their journey from Baldonnel's Aerodrome as it was relatively close to the Atlantic Ocean. Permission was granted and the two men arrived in Ireland and met with the Commandant of Baldonnel Aerodrome, Captain James C Fitzmaurice (1898–1965). In fact, Fitzmaurice had been part of one of those ten attempts in 1927 when he co-piloted the *Princess Xenia*, but atrocious weather off the coast of Galway, along with deteriorating visibility with every passing mile, forced his team to turn back and land in Kerry instead of New York.

The Germans invited Fitzmaurice to be a co-pilot. He had quite a career to commend him. A former Christian Brothers student, in Portlaoise, Fitzmaurice showed an early passion for army life. At sixteen years of age, he enlisted in the Seventh Battalion of the Royal Leinster Regiment, obliging his father to have him released for being three years below the minimum required age. The following year, in 1915, he enlisted in the British Army and ended up fighting in the trenches in France during the First World War. He was both wounded and recommended for a commission before fighting in the Battle of the Somme in 1916.

Promotions followed and in 1918, he was posted to the School of Military Aeronautics at Reading in England. That November, having completed his training as a fighter pilot, he was preparing to sail for France to re-enter the war in the air, but the armistice was announced. He continued to serve with the Royal Air Force (RAF) after the war until his resignation in August 1921 and held onto the RAF accent he had specifically cultivated to help his career in Britain, but that presumably won him few friends in Ireland.

In 1922, he switched 'teams', as it were, returning to the new state of Ireland to join the Irish Army's National Air Service. He was promoted to captain within the year and on 25 October 1925 became acting commandant in Baldonnel, where he was made second-in-command of the Irish Air Corps. He rose to the rank of commandant in September 1927.

The big day dawned on 12 April 1928. The large crowd that gathered in Baldonnel, including President WT Cosgrave, to cheer on the three pilots experienced a few moments of horror as they watched the *Bremen* taxi down the runway, heading straight for a lone, oblivious sheep. With 500 gallons of fuel onboard, any kind of a collision would end in a bonfire. It was Fitzmaurice who saved the day. Leaning across Köhl, who was in the pilot seat and unable to see the sheep, he grabbed the control stick to ease the plane into the air, clearing the animal before landing briefly and finally taking off properly.

A sometimes thrilling and terrifying thirty-six hours followed. There was the obligatory storm, and then Fitzmaurice found oil all over the cabin floor. They were forced 500 miles off course after all their compasses malfunctioned, with Fitzmaurice guessing that they must be near Newfoundland. Then another storm, an ice one, condemned them to fly blind until the morning of Friday, 13 April, when a welcome dash of daylight cut through the gloom, followed by the sight of snow-capped mountain peaks and deep valleys that suggested they were over North America. With fuel perilously low, they spent several hours searching for a safe place to land until Köhl brought the *Bremen* to rest upon a frozen reservoir on Greenly Island, between Newfoundland and Quebec. On landing, the plane broke through the ice, resulting in a dousing for all on board. The plane was out of action and the crew stranded, but they had done it – the first direct flight ever to America, a fine achievement.

Their subsequent exhilaration was surely tainted by the death, a few days later, of one of their rescuers, the American pilot Floyd Bennett (1890–1928) who was suffering from pneumonia following a previous crash. His health quickly deteriorated mid-rescue and he died in hospital on 25 April.

Five days later, the *Bremen* crew received a tumultuous welcome on the streets of New York. Two million people turned out to greet them and President Calvin Coolidge (1872–1933) rewarded them with the Distinguished Flying Cross, having pushed a bill through congress to allow him to present this prestigious American honour to the foreigner aviators.

It was also a big moment for *The Irish Times*, as its flamboyant editor RM 'Bertie' Smyllie (1893–1954) had given Captain Fitzmaurice four copies of the 12 April edition for the journey, thereby making it the first Irish news-paper to fly to America.

Back in Ireland, on 30 June, the three pilots were granted the Freedom of City of Dublin. On 3 July, they were driven down O'Connell Street, waving to the ecstatic crowds. According to the Catholic News Service, it was the biggest gathering ever on the street with people, desperate to glimpse the aviators, streaming into basements and restaurants on O'Connell Street. One imagines that it must have been a particularly proud moment for Fitzmaurice who was promoted to colonel.

Their names in the history books, they might have suspected that this was to be their finest moment. A few months later, in September, Baron Günther Von Hünefeld attempted to fly around the world but it ended in failure due to bad weather and his failing health. He died of stomach

The triumphant Bremen *crew being met by an ecstatic crowd on O'Connell Street.*

cancer in February 1929.

Herman Köhl lost his job with Deutsche Luft Hansa in 1935 and retired, aged just forty-seven. He chose to exchange the high life for a small farm in the south of Germany, taking refuge from the new ruling party, the Nationalist Socialists. His Catholicism and sense of morality made it impossible for him to show support for them in any way. Three years later, he died from kidney disease.

Captain James Fitzmaurice tried to keep the fires of glory burning, but it proved impossible. He dreamt of Ireland playing a central part in the rapidly developing aviation industry, but the government would not cooperate with his plans, leaving him feeling ignored and resentful. He almost achieved financial security for himself in making a deal with the Americans to sell them Junkers planes. However, the year was 1929 and the day that the forms were to be signed was the day that Wall Street fell, blowing many a dream to smithereens.

His final years were unhappy, following a messy divorce, and he found himself in straitened circumstances. He criticised the Irish for only celebrating the dead, a sentiment that he unknowingly proved in 1965 when his own death was commemorated with a state funeral with full military honours. A hero once again.

1970: Apollo XIII Crew

Described by astronaut Jim Lovell as 'the most successful failure', the crew of this space mission never actually made it to the Moon but they did make it to O'Connell Street in 1970.

Launched on 11 April 1970, this was the seventh crewed mission in America's Apollo space program and the astronauts, Jim Lovell (*b.* 1928), Fred Haise (*b.* 1933) and Jack Swigert (1931–82), were to be the third mission to land on the Moon. The Apollo spacecraft was actually two separate crafts connected by a tunnel – *Odyssey*, the command module or orbiter, and *Aquarius*, the small landing module.

Their amazing achievement lay in the fact that they made it back safely to Earth, following a potentially fatal accident fifty-six hours into their flight and 200,000 miles in space when one of their oxygen tanks exploded. They were forced them to evacuate *Odyssey* and squeeze into the *Aquarius* module, which was built to hold two men for two days, forty-five hours maximum. In fact, this lunar lifeboat would accommodate the three men for four days. But first it had to be charged up faster than advised since *Aquarius* would only have been switched on when they were close to landing on the moon. Apart from the cramped conditions, the astronauts had to contend with freezing temperatures as all power had to be saved for the return trip, thus rendering some of their food unfit for consumption. Water had to be rationed too, to six ounces per day, in case *Aquarius*'s hardware overheated and needed to be cooled down. The three men would lose a lot of weight, while Haise ended up with a lifelong kidney infection.

Next, they had to reroute their flight, that is, point the lunar module back towards Earth. Then they had to cobble together a filter in order to prevent their suffocating from the deadly build-up of carbon dioxide in the too-small-for-three-men *Aquarius*.

The 'homemade' filter was the result of pure innovation and genius from a team of NASA's best minds who could only use what was available on *Aquarius* and, naturally, they had to achieve a hundred per cent success as fast as they could since Lovell, Haise and Swigert were already starting to feel the debilitating effects of the poisonous atmosphere created by their own breath. Once accomplished, the CAPCOM (Capsule Communicator) Joe Kerwin (*b.* 1932) read out the instructions to *Aquarius*'s crew. There were nineteen steps, and it was reckoned it would take them an hour to coerce the likes of two LCG bags (liquid cooled garment), socks, the cover from a manual, hoses from space suits, grey duct tape and a bungee cord into a life-saving device. They had to be extra careful not to rip the bags as there were only two onboard.

Last, but by no means least, they had to exchange *Aquarius*, which had no heat shield, for *Odyssey* once more, just before re-entry into the earth's atmosphere at a temperature of 5,000 degrees. This would cause a temporary black-out of three minutes with Mission Control. As they released the lunar module, CAPCOM Kerwin was moved to say aloud, 'Farewell, *Aquarius*, and we thank you.' All over the world, people stopped to watch what happened next. Less than ten minutes from earth, Jim Lovell and his crew performed their final checks, taking the time to thank everyone at Houston for their work and support. And then all went quiet.

The crew's relatives and colleagues held their breath as their respective television screens and monitors flickered in silence, counting down the predicted three minutes, and then some.

Mission Control found themselves in a new and terrifying situation as the seconds ticked by without a sound from *Odyssey*. After three and a half minutes, they were in unprecedented territory with a growing conviction that something had gone horribly wrong, but all they could do was sit and wait while the CAPCOM attempted to make contact: '*Odyssey*, Houston, standing by, over.'

Ninety seconds over the predicted three minutes, Mission Control erupted at the sound of Jim Lovell's voice, 'Okay, Joe.' They had made it.

Afterwards, a NASA investigation board declared the explosion to be the work of a spark from an exposed wire in the oxygen tank that was, in turn, judged to be both a manufacturer's and a testing error.

This is the expedition that inspired Ron Howard's 1995 film, *Apollo 13*, starring Tom Hanks (Jim Lovell), Bill Paxton (Fred Haise) and Kevin Bacon (Jack Swigert).

Thirty-eight-year-old John ('Jack') Swigert was making his debut flight. He was invited to join Apollo XIII's crew just forty-eight hours before the launch after module pilot Ken Mattingly (*b*. 1936) was exposed to German measles. Swigert would be the one to utter that immortal line, 'Houston, we've had a problem.' In the 1995 film, Tom Hanks, as Jim Lovell, gets the big line which was tweaked to, 'Houston, we have a problem.'

Plans to celebrate the fiftieth anniversary of this homecoming had to be postponed due to the 2020 outbreak of the Covid-19 virus. It seems that the crew of this particular mission should forget about making any kind of plans, even fifty years later.

Once home, President Nixon sent them on what was called the Aquarius European Presidential Goodwill Tour, lending them a presidential jet. The company of five – the three astronauts along with wives Marilyn Lovell and Mary Haise – visited six countries in fifteen days for a tight schedule that ensured that the Haises could get back to their three-month-old son as fast as they could.

They arrived into Dublin Airport at 1.20pm on Tuesday, 13 October where they were greeted by the US Ambassador John DJ Moore (1910–88)

The Apollo XIII crew receiving a warm welcome on O'Connell Street in 1970.

and 300 dignitaries and spectators. From there, a white sportscar took them on a slow drive into the city centre via O'Connell Street, en route to a press conference at the Intercontinental Hotel in Ballsbridge. The American flags were still in place from President Nixon's visit a couple of weeks previously.

The following day they went to St Patrick's Cathedral to thank Dean Victor G Griffin (1924–2017) for setting up an all-night prayer vigil during their precarious journey back to earth. That evening, they attended a party in Áras an Uachtaráin, in the Phoenix Park, where they drank champagne and sang 'Happy Birthday' to eighty-eight-year-old President Éamon de Valera. They didn't come empty-handed, making the Irish president a gift of an inscribed piece of the heat shield and mission patch, two of the items that helped save their lives. This birthday present went on show, in 1985, in the Presidential Room of the National Museum of Ireland (NMI) as part of their collection of possessions belonging to Irish presidents.

They also visited Cork Opera House and Limerick where they ended up being mobbed by enthusiastic autograph hunters.

AMERICAN PRESIDENTS
John Fitzgerald Kennedy

In 1847, at the height of the Irish Famine, a New Ross man boarded a ship for America, hoping to make a new life from himself. Three generations later, the man's great-grandson would visit Ireland, stopping off in New Ross for a cup of tea and a slice of cake with his New Ross cousins.

President John Fitzgerald Kennedy (1917–63) flew into Dublin airport on 26 June 1963, a highly anticipated trip for all involved. Not only was this a visit of an extremely popular president who continually played up his Irish roots and was the youngest man ever voted into the office, this was also the first visit to Ireland by a sitting American president and America's

A beaming JFK acknowledging his legions of fans on O'Connell Street.

first Catholic Irish American president at that.

It was unfortunate that First Lady Jacqueline (1929–94) could not be with him owing to a difficult birth that had ended with the tragic loss of baby Patrick. In fact, Kennedy was not in the best of health himself, suffering from serious back troubles and Addison's disease, which causes extreme fatigue, weight loss, lack of appetite and hyperpigmentation of the skin. He had been diagnosed with the disease in 1947 at the age of thirty. Looking at film footage online, he does look rather slender beneath his immaculate suit, while that famous suntan had less to do with the sun than with the disease's effect on his skin. Two and a half years in office had brought him a great deal of stress, professionally and physically, and privately he would have been grieving the loss of his son.

He and his entourage flew in following their visit to Berlin, which had ended on a high note with Kennedy delivering his '*Ich bin ein Berliner*' speech. However, this was nowhere near the ecstatic welcome he received in Ireland. According to those who accompanied him – staff, two sisters and a sister-in-law – he had not been so relaxed in a long time, a view shared by historian Arthur Schlesinger (1888–1965) who wrote that Kennedy was 'more completely himself' throughout his four-day Irish tour.

The motorcade went down O'Connell Street, followed by secret service and dignitaries. The footage can be seen in RTÉ's archives. There are glimpses of the aging Irish President de Valera sitting upright in the back of the open-topped car, while beside him is Kennedy, on his feet, acknowledging the cheering crowds. RTÉ's commentator remarks that the young president looks at ease and reflects that the spools of ticker tape made O'Connell Street look like Wall Street. Actually, people were throwing CIÉ bus ticket rolls because there was no ticker tape to be had.

This wasn't Kennedy's first visit. Sixteen years earlier, he had toured Ireland for three weeks, stopping of in New Ross, but this was his first visit as President. He spent his last night with President de Valera and his wife, the poet and writer Sinéad (1878–1975). After dinner, the poet read aloud a poem she had written for the Irish exile. Kennedy was so taken by it that he scribbled it down on a place mat, learned it off by heart and, the following day, used it as part of his farewell and final speech, in which he promised to return.

He told his aides that, for him, the highlight of the trip had been the laying of the wreaths at Arbour Hill military cemetery in Dublin, where he had been hugely impressed with the 36th Cadet Class who had provided his guard of honour – so much so that he requested a video of the event but none proved sufficient. Since the 36th had been commissioned in July 1963 and the cadets gone to their various bases, the 37th made an early start on their ceremonial drills and it was they who provided the footage. And they would provide a lot more.

The President never came back to Ireland, being gunned down a mere five months later in Dallas, Texas. The following day, the commandment of the Cadet School in the Curragh received a phone call informing him that

Jacqueline Kennedy had requested that the Irish government send over the Irish cadets to form a guard of honour once more for the President, this time at his funeral on 25 November 1963.

On 15 June 1967, former First Lady Jacqueline Kennedy arrived in Ireland with her two children, nine-year-old Caroline and six-year-old John, for a month-long holiday. Big crowds, which may well have cheered on her husband four years earlier, turned out to welcome her wherever she went.

Richard Nixon

Seven years after JFK's visit, another American President did not have quite as good a reception. The thirty-seventh President of the United States, Richard Nixon's (1913–94) Air Force One touched down at Shannon Airport at 5pm on Saturday, 3 October 1970, for his three day visit. Presumably, he was on a high from the previous day when he had experienced a thunderous welcome in Madrid, as he sat alongside General Franco. His visit to England, the morning of 3 October, necessitated a massive security detail and, then, he and the First Lady Patricia Nixon (1912–93) arrived in Ireland to be met by Taoiseach Jack Lynch (1917–99) and his wife Máirín (1916–2004), amongst others.

Like Kennedy, Nixon had Irish roots, as did, Pat, his wife, and an ancestral home to visit. His mother's ancestors were Quakers and buried in the Quaker cemetery in Hodgestown, near Timahoe in County Kildare, where he was received warmly and spoke about his presidential desire to bring peace to all the world. A poignant desire, certainly, as he was looking for a way to get American soldiers out of Vietnam and bring to an end their part in a most unpopular war that had begun in 1955 (and would not end until 1975).

Monday, 5 October was his final day and was a busy one involving a stop-off at the Phoenix Park to meet President de Valera, followed by lunch with the Taoiseach at Dublin Castle. En route to the castle, the crowd lined the streets just as they had for Kennedy but not everyone was there to cheer on this on particular president. Nixon stood just as Kennedy did, through the open sunroof of his bulletproof car, waving and smiling before suddenly ducking down to avoid an egg that had been fired straight at him.

In 2019, *The Journal* interviewed Máirín de Burca who was arrested along with her two colleagues for egging Nixon's car in protest against America's involvement in the Vietnam War. A lifelong activist and campaigner, de Burca was working as a Sinn Féin secretary in 1970 and was horrified by news footage of what was happening in Vietnam. There were plenty of protests taking place across America and de Burca wanted to play her part too. On hearing that Nixon was to visit Ireland, she recognised her opportunity. There had been some talk of throwing stones before settling for eggs as they did not want to hurt anyone. Her two colleagues were future IRA-member-turned-investigative-journalist twenty-year-old Martin O'Hagan (1950–2001) and forty-one-year-old Richard Bannister.

They took up their positions at three vantage points and each managed to hit the car, obliging Nixon to hunker down by his wife, both still smiling as they got out at Dublin Castle. In fact, de Burca had a lucky escape. When the guards caught her, she found herself the target of an angry group of women who screamed, 'Lynch her!' with one woman attempting to slap her.

The trio ended up in the District Court in front of a judge who was infamous for his tough sentences but, nevertheless, shared their animosity for Richard Nixon resulting in each of them being fined a minimal £1 or £2.

After lunch, the Nixons were driven up O'Connell Street on their way to Dublin airport for their flight home. There were plenty more protestors with banners and boos and, apparently, plenty more eggs too, though none would make their mark. Of course, today we appreciate that those protests were fine rain when compared to the storms that were coming four years later, culminating in Nixon's resignation following the Watergate Scandal.

Ronald Reagan

The GPO was the focus point for those protesting the visit of the for-tieth American President to Ireland. Former movie star Ronald Reagan (1911–2004) arrived in Ireland on Friday 1 June 1984, for a four-day trip that included a visit to his ancestral home in Ballyporeen, County Tipperary. The locals turned out to give him a fine welcome while elsewhere thousands of Irish people raised their voices in dissent in a nationwide demonstration called Ring Around Reagan.

Five thousand people gathered in front of the GPO and had themselves a protest party with music and song. Amongst the ordinary citizens from north and south of the border were priests, nuns and public representatives standing together in a united show of contempt for America's foreign policy. Slogans on various banners ranged from 'Coleraine CND Anti-Nuclear Group' and 'Defend Nicaragua and Cuba' to 'El Savador Support Group'.

Whatever about the storms that Nixon stirred up for himself in later years, it was left to the forty-second President of the United States, Bill Clinton (*b.* 1946) to take a walk up O'Connell Street while an actual storm, Ophelia, was making herself felt. It was almost 2.30pm on 16 October 2017 when a passer-by videoed the large black armoured car pulling up across from the O'Connell Monument. The street was largely empty of traffic and pedestrians as the wind was starting to rear up and most folk had followed the advice to head home.

Clinton was in Dublin to receive an honorary doctorate from Dublin City University in recognition of 'his leadership in building and consolidating peace and reconciliation on the island of Ireland'. This was just one of several visits to the area. In August 2004, Clinton was in Eason's, O'Connell Street, to sign copies of his biography *My Life*. Hundreds queued up outside ahead of his 9am arrival.

Barack Obama

If the forty-fourth President of the United States, Barack Obama (b.1961), did not actually stand on O'Connell Street, he stood near it and did the next best thing which was to reference 'your great liberator' Daniel O'Connell, in his speech to the 25,000-strong crowd that gathered at College Green. It was part of a rather short but busy twenty-four-hour visit to Ireland that he made with wife Michelle (*b*. 1964) in May 2011. The President spoke about the former slave and abolitionist Frederick Douglass's visit to Dublin in 1845, and the great friendship that was forged between Douglass and O'Connell. Not surprising, the reference produced a roar of approval.

The forty-fifth President Donald Trump (*b*. 1946) steered clear of Dublin altogether in his visit to Ireland in 2019, a wise move considering the thousands of Irish people who turned out to protest his presidency and

O'Connell Street and the Garden of Remembrance bore witness to protests and a giant inflatable model of Donald Trump in a nappy during the American president's 2019 visit to Ireland.

his visit by marching up O'Connell Street. However, a blimp, a six-meter-high inflatable model of Trump in a nappy, was floated above the crowds at the Garden of Remembrance. 2019 was a busy year for the blimp which had already accompanied anti-Trump protestors on marches throughout America, South America and London, from where it was especially flown in by Uplift activists.

FUNERAL PROCESSIONS

Thanks to its proximity to Glasnevin Cemetery, the street has seen many funerals, playing a capital role in the final journey of some of the nation's biggest names, although not all were famous.

The English writer GR Smith visited the GPO in 1859 to inspect its Dead-Letter Office and stayed in a nearby hotel. On Sunday morning, he and his English colleagues were intrigued by a procession slowly making its way down Sackville Street. It was quite a spectacle, with six men taking the lead in green morning coats, green hats, brown knickers and grey stockings, smoking pipes as they went. Behind them, two men carried a pole about 17 feet long, to which two large red handkerchiefs had been tied to secure a heavy-looking box. Then came a man with a donkey cart, carrying three women, all wearing colourful shawls and, behind them again, Smith counted between forty and fifty men, women and children. The English visitors were so fascinated that they asked what the men were carrying, discovering that it was no ordinary box. Rather, it was a coffin containing a dead child; the colourful procession was the funeral party.

The explanation, however, did not fill them with pity for the child and its family. Instead, they thought it highly inappropriate to see such a private moment on 'grotesque' display on such an important street.

Perhaps Elizabeth Shannon would agree with Mr Smith. The wife of the American ambassador confessed in her diary that the Irish attitude to death and illness made her shiver. According to her, not a week goes by without a photograph of the 'Weeping Widow' in the national papers, the bigger the funeral, the better. She also writes about Irish politicians dropping everything to attend and be seen at funerals in order to curry votes at the next election.

When Daniel Murray, the immensely popular Archbishop of Dublin and co-founder of St Vincent's Hospital, died in 1852, his funeral received a brief mention in Elizabeth Grant's 1851–6 diary. She and her daughter attended the funeral mass in Christ Church Cathedral, describing it as long but 'good'. After the mass, they followed a huge crowd to Sackville Street, which was crammed 'from end to end' with mourners.

Michael Collins's funeral drew thousands of mourners to O'Connell Street.

Michael Collins

Would Elizabeth Shannon and GR Smith have baulked at what took place on O'Connell Street on 28 August 1922, when approximately half a million Irish men, women and children gathered to bid farewell to thirty-two year old Michael Collins, following his killing six days earlier?

In her memoir, the Countess of Fingall, a friend of Hazel Lavery, describes meeting Collins at a dinner the night before he drove to Cork. The dinner, hosted by Senator and writer Sir Horace Plunkett (1854–1932), was in honour of the Irish playwright George Bernard Shaw (1856–1950) and his wife, Charlotte Payne-Townshend (1857–1943). Hazel Lavery rang to ask Sir Horace if the Bernard Shaws might like to meet Michael Collins and, of course, they did. However, the dinner party, which also included WT Cosgrave, future president of Ireland, was subdued with the countess confessing to her diary that she found Collins 'not at all an eloquent man', perhaps blaming him for the dullness of the dinner. In hindsight, Collins was probably in mourning for the fifty-one-year-old President Arthur Griffith who had died on 12 August from a cerebral haemorrhage and heart failure.

Oliver St John Gogarty, who championed both Collins and Griffith, wrote in his memoir, 'What an unlucky shake-hands de Valera gives! He shakes hands to speed Collins and Griffith to London. They are dead within the year.'

The countess describes reading about Collins's murder in her newspaper, the morning of Wednesday, 23 August, as she sat with Mrs Shaw. A little while later, they were joined by Hazel Lavery – rumoured to be having an affair with Collins – who declared that she knew he would die after he appeared in her dreams, his face covered in blood. The countess accompanied Hazel to St Vincent's Hospital where Collins's body was lying in state in the mortuary chapel of the Sisters of Charity. He had been embalmed, at the government's request, by his good friend Oliver St John Gogarty.

Lady Hazel Lavery was rumoured to be having an affair with Michael Collins.

Four men in uniform stood guard over him, while candles were lit at his head and feet. Their fallen leader was in full uniform with a pristine white bandage around his head, lending him, according to the countess, 'beauty and dignity' in death.

The countess had had to stop Hazel Lavery from putting on widow's weeds for their visit and then had to order her home, leaving Collins's fiancée Kitty Kiernan (1893–1945) to her rightful position as chief mourner.

The body was taken to City Hall and from there to the Pro-Cathedral, on the Sunday evening, for the Requiem High Mass on Monday, 28 August. Hazel Lavery's husband John, the celebrated artist, painted the scene from

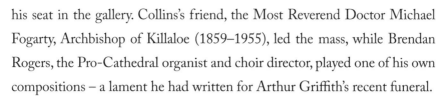

his seat in the gallery. Collins's friend, the Most Reverend Doctor Michael Fogarty, Archbishop of Killaloe (1859–1955), led the mass, while Brendan Rogers, the Pro-Cathedral organist and choir director, played one of his own compositions – a lament he had written for Arthur Griffith's recent funeral.

John Lavery's painting, which can be seen in the Hugh Lane Gallery, shows standing room only in the cathedral. Apart from family and friends, the cathedral was crammed with government officials, politicians, civil servants and representatives from universities and groups such as the Irish Farmers' Association.

The funeral can be watched online. Six horses pull the carriage that bears the coffin, covered in the Tricolour, and just in front are two cars completely covered in floral bouquets for the grave. As they approach O'Connell Street, a strong breeze materialises and appears to play with the flag, not actually blowing it off the coffin but whipping it up all the same. This burst of movement is highlighted by the stillness of the mourners and spectators. Children stand with their hats in their hands, although one little girl drops hers as the soldiers march by, darting forward to grab it before jumping back in line. Women are crying, the shock and grief is palpable.

The procession, which was several miles long, took several hours to reach Glasnevin Cemetery where General Richard Mulcahy (1886–1971), the Minister for Defence and Collins's successor as Commander-in-Chief of the Irish Republican Army, delivered the funeral oration.

Margaret Pearse

Politician, and mother to the 1916 revolutionaries Pádraig and Willie, Margaret Pearse (*b.* 1857) died on 22 April 1932 and was the first woman to be given a state funeral.

She married the monumental sculptor James Pearse (1839–1900) in 1877 and they had four children, two girls and two boys, all born while the

The funeral cortège of Margaret Pearse stops briefly outside the GPO.

family lived at 27 Great Brunswick Street. They moved to Sandymount in 1888, where the children were inspired by Margaret's aunt, a frequent visitor, to take a keen interest in the Irish language and culture. Widowed in 1900, Margaret maintained James's sculpture business while also devoting herself to her children's passions. When Pádraig, her eldest, set up St Enda's school in Rathfarnham eight years later, she got involved and became its popular housekeeper and matron. In 1916, just before their march to the GPO, she sewed medals on the students' uniforms.

In 1917, she became one of the vice-presidents in Cumann na mBan (The Irish Women's Council) with Countess Markievicz at the helm.

Presumably, the fate of her two boys inspired her to join Sinn Féin after the Easter Rising and in 1920 she stood as a successful candidate for Rathmines in the Poor Law Elections. Meanwhile, Dublin City Council passed a resolution to rename Great Brunswick Street as Pearse Street.

The following year, she was elected to Dáil Éireann where she continued to be inspired by her sons' legacy. For example, she fervently opposed the Anglo-Irish Treaty, as did all the female TDs, and made a speech contradicting the suggestion that her son would have supported it:

> I rise to support the motion of our President for the rejection of the Treaty. My reasons for doing so are various, but my first reason for doing so I would like to explain here today is my son's account. It has been said here on several occasions that Patrick Pearse would have accepted this Treaty. I deny it. As his mother I deny it, and, on his account, I will not accept it.

Defeated in the 1922 elections, she threw her support behind those who rejected the Treaty, and remained in Sinn Féin until 1926 when she co-founded Fianna Fáil with Éamon de Valera, whom she perhaps saw as a noble successor to Pádraig.

Not surprisingly, her constant promotion of her boys as the real heroes of the Rising was a problem for some of her colleagues in Cumann na mBan. Kathleen Clarke (1878–1972), in particular, disagreed with what she felt was a skewed narrative of the events in the GPO, at the expense of her husband Tom's contribution and legacy. At their convention in 1922, someone suggested dismissing Margaret Pearse from the council.

In 1924, seventy-year-old Margaret sailed to New York to raise funds for St Enda's, which she continued to run with her daughters, Mary Margaret and Mary Brigid, while also voicing her allegiance to de Valera's Republic of Ireland. At one point, she boasted of turning down Michael Collins's 'bribe', that is, his offer to subsidise her school. She spoke about her sons at every opportunity, calling herself 'the proudest mother in Ireland'.

In 1931, when de Valera founded *The Irish Press* newspaper, it was Margaret who pressed the button to launch the printing of its very first issue.

On Tuesday, 26 April 1932, thousands turned out to bid farewell to surely one of the most famous mothers in Irish history. Her coffin was brought from City Hall, where she had been lying in state, down O'Connell Street in a four-horse drawn carriage, stopping outside the GPO for a minute's silence before continuing to Glasnevin Cemetery where President Éamon de Valera gave the funeral oration.

Thirty-six years later, her eldest child, Senator Margaret Mary Pearse (*b.* 1878) was accorded the same privilege of a state funeral when she died in 1968.

Lillie Connolly

The second woman to receive a state funeral was the sixty-eight-year-old widow of the revolutionary leader and socialist James, Lillie Connolly (*née* Reynolds 1867–1938). Born in Wicklow, Lillie ended up in Dublin working as a governess to a family in Merrion Square. Meanwhile, the Scottish-Irish Connolly was stationed in Ireland with the British Army, having been signed up by his family at just fourteen years old. They met after Connolly missed his tram and she flashed him a sympathetic smile. He struck up a conversation with her and, at some point, suggested that she come visit him when he returned to Edinburgh, which she did, marrying him soon after in April 1890. Over the next few years, they had six daughters and a son. It was not an easy life; they were often penniless, while James was continually frustrated in his political ambitions.

They returned to Ireland in May 1896 when James was hired by the Dublin Socialist Party.

In September 1903, he decided to try his luck in America, travelling ahead to secure employment and save for boats tickets for Lillie and the children. Finally, in August 1904, the family booked their passage. The day before they set sail, their eldest, thirteen-year-old Mona, was fatally burned whilst babysitting her younger sister in a friend's house when her apron

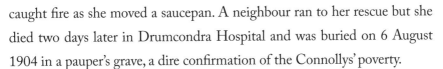

caught fire as she moved a saucepan. A neighbour ran to her rescue but she died two days later in Drumcondra Hospital and was buried on 6 August 1904 in a pauper's grave, a dire confirmation of the Connollys' poverty.

A devastated Lillie and the rest of the children sailed to America the following week. Instead of a joyous family reunion, Lillie had to tell James that his beloved Mona was dead. Six years later, James decided to return to Ireland, where he got a job in Belfast as James Larkin's right-hand man in the Irish Transport and General Workers' Union (ITGWU) and attempted to get into politics. Lillie set up home and was presumably grateful when her two daughters, Nora and Ina, found work as seamstresses.

In 1911, according to the consensus, Lillie was forty-three years old. Of her six surviving children, only eighteen-year-old Nora was working, as a dressmaker, and her youngest child, Fiona, was just four years of age. She held the fort while her husband travelled to wherever he was needed, including Dublin.

Throughout all the trouble of the 1913 Lockout and those intervening years leading to the takeover of the GPO, it was Lillie who tended to her children and never wavered in her wholehearted support of her husband's ventures. When her husband ended up in Mountjoy Prison in 1913, Lillie marched to the lord lieutenant's mansion in the Phoenix Park to plead for an intercession in her husband's case.

James Connolly had embarked on a hunger strike, following in the footsteps of imprisoned suffragettes, all demanding the right to free speech. An ardent feminist as well as a socialist, he could ably devote himself to his passions knowing that Lillie was taking care of everything else. Some sources describe her demanding that the lord lieutenant at the time, the Seventh Earl of Aberdeen, John Hamilton-Gordon (1847–1934) have her husband released. She may have felt emboldened by the fact that the earl and James Connolly shared a native city in Edinburgh.

And, maybe it was Lillie who arranged for Countess Markievicz to take in Connolly when he left Mountjoy in a weakened state. As Easter 1916 approached, Lillie moved her family into Countess Markievicz's house. Afterwards, she managed to visit her wounded husband twice before his execution in Kilmainham Gaol.

She outlived her husband by twenty-two years, dying at home, at 36 Belgrave Square, after a long illness. According to *The Irish Press*, she was a favourite with the children in her neighbourhood and one of her wreaths was signed from 'The Children of Belgrave Square'.

Thousands lined the streets to pay their respects. Her coffin bore the Tricolour and the flag of the Irish Citizen Army. Mourners included men who had trained under James Connolly. All aspects of her husband's career were represented in the huge funeral cortège that followed the Workers' Union of Ireland band.

Her coffin departed Mount Argus's Church in a horse-drawn carriage and passed the GPO on its way to Glasnevin Cemetery, in a procession that included President de Valera, former president WT Cosgrave and his wife Louisa (1882–1959), and future Tánaiste Frank Aiken.

Kathleen Clarke

The last woman to receive a state funeral in Ireland was Kathleen Clarke, Tom Clarke's widow, on 3 October 1972. A founding member of Cumann na mBan, she went on to become the first female lord mayor of Dublin (1939–41).

Éamon de Valera

Born George de Valero in New York in 1882, to an Irish mother, Catherine ('Kate') Coll (1856–1932), and Juan Vivion de Valera (1854–85/6), a Spanish artist, the future president of Ireland Éamon de Valera arrived here as

The funeral of Irish president Éamon de Valera.

a two-and-a-half-year-old toddler with his uncle Ned. No proof has ever been found of his parents' marriage but his mother told him that his father died *c.* 1885, leaving them in straitened circumstances. She did not send for him after her second wedding in the 1880s, leaving his upbringing to her mother and family in Limerick.

A diligent student, 'Dev' ended up in Blackrock College, in Dublin, where he fell in love with rugby and went on to play for Munster in 1905. He became a mathematics teacher and taught in various schools including Carysfort Teacher Training College for women. After briefly considering joining the priesthood, he joined the Gaelic League instead in 1908, taking up Irish classes at the Leinster College in Parnell Square and falling for his teacher. Four years older than her student, Sinéad Flanagan (1878–1975) was from Balbriggan and went on to become a prolific children's writer. They married two years later and had five sons and two daughters, losing one son, Brian, at twenty, to injuries incurred from a horse-riding accident in the Phoenix Park.

From 1916 onwards, Éamon de Valera embarked on a new vocation, that of a highly influential political figure in Ireland. This included being temporarily sentenced to death for his part in the Easter Rising and also being imprisoned in England – badges of honour for the Irish American. He returned to Ireland and played a leading role in the War of Independence, sending Michael Collins and Arthur Griffith to London to discuss terms for a treaty that de Valera rejected on their return – a rejection that tore Ireland in half, family by family.

He led the anti-Treaty Sinn Féin until 1926 when he cofounded a new political party, Fianna Fáil, enabling him to take his seat in Dáil Éireann.

Under the new constitution in 1937, de Valera succeeded WT Cosgrave as President of the Executive Council. He was taoiseach three times between 1937 and 1959, the year he was elected President of Ireland and thereby obliged to resign from the party he had led for thirty-three years, handing over power to Seán Lemass. De Valera served two terms of presidency, from 1959 to 1973, finally retiring at ninety years of age. He died two years later, on 29 August, from cardiac failure and bronchial pneumonia. Sinéad had died eight months earlier, on the eve of their 65th wedding anniversary.

His body lay in state for two days in St Patrick's Hall, Dublin Castle before being taken by gun carriage to the Pro-Cathedral. The funeral took place on Tuesday, 2 September, and over 200,000 people turned up to watch the huge procession of family, friends, political leaders, diplomats, veterans of the 1916 Rising and even Princess Grace of Monaco make its way, in the sunshine, to Glasnevin Cemetery via O'Connell Street.

There is plenty of footage online, with one British commentor suggesting that four generations of Irish people should consider the effect that 'this lone Promethean figure' had on their lives. In Ancient Greek mythology, Prometheus incurs the wrath of the gods by stealing their fire for the human race.

Of course, he had his detractors as all politicians do. For many, his offering Germany condolences on the suicide of Adolf Hitler was bewildering, although he probably felt it was necessary in order to emphasise, and therefore safeguard, Irish neutrality during the Second World War. Like him or not, his passion for Ireland could not be faulted. Even before Hitler's suicide, the British government worried that de Valera was forming close links with Germany's Nazi ambassador to Ireland, Eduard Hempel (1887–1972). Certainly, de Valera was no favourite of British Prime Minister Winston Churchill (1874–1965) who only ever viewed him as a 'terrorist' and never forgave him for his belligerent response to the 1921 Treaty.

At Glasnevin, he was placed into the grave alongside his wife and son and there was no funeral oration because he had not wanted one, preferring to be remembered for what he did, not for what someone would say about him.

Alfie Byrne

Many hold that Alfie Byrne would have made a worthy president, if only for the fact that he was, and still is, the only Irish politician to have been elected an MP, a TD, a senator and lord mayor of Dublin.

The second eldest of eight children, he was born on St Patrick's Day in 1882 to Thomas and wife Frances (Tom and Fanny) at 36 Seville Place, just off the North Strand in Dublin, Alfie liked to call himself a third-generation Dubliner because his father and grandfather had been born a mile away from where he grew up. Meanwhile, his mother's grandfather was Colonel Dowman, a Protestant soldier in the British Army. His father and paternal grandfather also worked in Dublin Port, where Tom was presumably a 'Jack of all trades', having several job titles attached to his name: engineer, docker and ship's pilot. However, after getting involved with the trade union, Tom lost his job in 1895, obliging him to exchange their house for a two-roomed house on Lower Oriel Street and send the two oldest

Alfie Byrne is still the only Irish politician to have been elected as MP, TD, senator, and Lord Mayor of Dublin.

boys out to work, thirteen-year-old Alfie and his brother Lar.

Alfie was a natural grafter and quickly found work selling programmes outside the Tivoli Theatre on Burgh Quay as well as serving an apprenticeship as a mechanic for a bicycle shop in Dawson Street, a street that would become very dear to him later on.

By 1901, he was working in a local pub owned by his future father-in-law Thomas Heagney. It could be said that it was here, behind the bar, that he acquired the skills necessary to be a successful politician: soothing troubled waters and maintaining friendly relations with all, while also knowing when to take charge of a situation.

Later on, he moved out of the cramped family home to live above a pub he managed near the Four Courts. In 1908, thanks to his disciplined frugality – and perhaps Thomas Heagney – his savings enabled him to buy his own pub, The Verdon in Talbot Street. He also joined the United Irish League and became a treasurer for his local branch.

Two years later, in 1910, he married Elizabeth (Cissie) Heagney (c. 1888–1954) and decided to run for Dublin City Council. The United Irish League chose him as their candidate for the North Dock Ward which was then the biggest working-class district in Dublin. In 1914, he became an alderman for Dublin Corporation and the following year, as a member of the Irish Parliamentary Party (IPP), he was elected Member of Parliament (MP) for Dublin Harbour.

The Irish Times columnist Frank McNally describes how Byrne, a gifted orator in The House of Commons, momentarily lost his cool in May 1916 after Prime Minster Herbert Henry Asquith (1852–1928) read out the number of British soldiers (521) who had been wounded or killed during the Rising. Normally opposed to violence, Byrne cried out, 'You ought to shoot (Edward) Carson for that!'

In 1917, he was the only member of the IPP to attend the funeral of hunger striker and former Lord Mayor of Cork Thomas Ashe (b. 1885). Although sympathetic to the likes of Pearse and Connolly, Alfie Byrne was a pacifist and a huge admirer of Charles Stewart Parnell, leader of the Irish Parliamentary Party, who preferred the conservative political approach over guns and bloodshed.

Sinn Féin's increased popularity after the Rising saw Byrne lose his parliamentary seat in 1918. However, four years later, he was returned as an independent and was re-elected to the Dáil for Dublin's Mid constituency.

From 1923 to 1928, he served as TD for Dublin North and was also elected to Seanad Éireann for six years. He became lord mayor of Dublin in October 1930, the first of his record-breaking ten separate terms, and was a hugely popular figure on the streets of Dublin. The job came with a secretary and steward as well as a change of address. Yards away from where he served his mechanic apprenticeship, Byrne and his family moved into the Mansion House, with Alfie ordering building repairs costing £5,000. He also took on a second secretary along with a chauffeur and three maids.

A legendary man about town, he earned his nickname, 'The Shaking Hand of Dublin', thanks to his habit of greeting pretty much everyone he met, giving sweets to the children and an extended hand to the adults. His biographer, Trevor White, describes him as a dedicated problem-solver. For instance, when the singer Luke Kelly's (1940–84) father approached Byrne after a fire devasted his home, Byrne had the Kelly family relocated within hours.

Locals described him as 'always being there' and as a result his popularity as mayor was not surprising. There was no need to make an appointment. An average day saw him deal with up to fifty people in his office in the Mansion House, where no one was turned away. In his first year, he answered 15,000 letters. A journalist spent some time with him in 1931 and, within an hour, had watched Byrne accept 'seventeen invitations to public dinners, one invitation to public entertainment and eight invitations to public functions'. After that, he dictated forty-three letters to those seeking employment. Of course, something had to give and he was a largely absent father to his eight children.

Neither was he everyone's favourite. For instance, Seán Lemass (1899–1971) denounced him for arriving into the Dáil chamber, dressed in formal wear, to make a plea for the impoverished of Dublin on his way to a society ball.

In any case, he did his best by Dublin's poor. During a Dáil debate in

1923, he asked the minister for Local Government if he knew that thousands of citizens were living in rat-infested basements before asking to hear the Government's Housing Policy for 1923–4. A serious lack of housing for rich and poor alike was blamed on the high building costs. Throughout 1922 and 1923, Alfie Byrne suggested that the government provide grants to private builders to encourage them to get cracking on 30,000 desperately needed cottages.

But then there was 'that' photograph. In 1934, Byrne was photographed with Eoin O'Duffy and his Blueshirts in the Mansion House and it appears that all were making the fascist salute though the lord mayor looks somewhat sheepish with his hand dangling half-heartedly overhead.

Professionally, he proved just as sociable. He was the first lord mayor of Dublin to visit North America in forty years and was declared a 'Champion Showman' in the *New York Times*, while in Toronto he was granted the Freedom of the City.

At the risk of losing support from patriotic Dubliners, he attended the 1936 funeral of King George V (b. 1877), the only Irish politician to do so. He believed in maintaining a favourable relationship with England and was known to show off a portrait of Queen Victoria in the Mansion House. In an interview for *Pathe Gazette*, which can be seen online, he is seated in a garden wearing his Lord Mayor chain – the same one, he emphasises, that Daniel O'Connell wore. The purpose of the interview, he explains, is to address the question that is frequently posed to him on his travels across the water: 'What is the matter with Ireland?' He assures his listeners that there is no serious animosity between the people of Ireland and Britain and that he sees the potential of everyone working together to increase prosperity for all. However, he believes that the Irish border between North and South should be removed, referring to it as a 'festering sore'. It is his life's ambition to bring people together, have them think about the unemployed, and be filled with a shared desire to dismantle the border as it is so expensive to keep two parliaments open in the one country.

In 1938, there was every reason to believe that he might become Ireland's first president, but it was not to be. Nominations opened up on 14 April and various names were bandied about in the press. On 20 April, *The Irish Times* ran a piece suggesting that Alfie Byrne would be perfect for the job, a sentiment that was shared by many, including the man himself. However, this article may have spurred on a meeting that ensured that Byrne would never be president. Éamon de Valera quietly met with his rival WT Cosgrave to discuss potential candidates, quickly concluding that the Gaelic scholar Dr Douglas Hyde would be the only nomination; perhaps real history was made when the three leading political parties, Fianna Fáil, Fine Gael and the Labour Party were in complete agreement with this. Draw your own conclusions, but the man who became Ireland's first president was quiet and not flamboyant in any way and was nowhere near as popular a figure as Alfie Byrne.

In hindsight, that photograph with his raised hand alongside the Blueshirts might have hampered any presidential prospects.

He died four days short of his seventy-fourth birthday from cancer of the oesophagus and was given a state funeral, which had a huge turnout. The cortège, made up of 150 cars, brought O'Connell Street to a standstill for over twenty minutes whilst thousands lined the streets all the way to Glasnevin Cemetery. Taoiseach John A Costello (1891–1976) led the tributes with the members of the Dáil observing a short silence to mark his passing. Other tributes included a telegram sent to Cissie from Robert F Wagner Jnr (1910–91), the Mayor of New York.

Afterword

The conversation about rejuvenating today's O'Connell Street began as far back as 1998 and has proven to be a challenging topic. Different groups feel invested, either emotionally or financially, in this high-profile area, resulting in divisions being laid down between those who would prefer permanent reminders of the past and those who believe the way forward is to, where possible, start anew.

We remember the GPO staff preferring to stay put amidst construction work in 2019. The ties that bind cannot be trivialised.

On 1 April 2021, the Dublin Chamber of Commerce invited members to an online presentation by Ed Dobbs, the Development Manager of Hammerson, entitled 'Reviving the Heart of Dublin, the Future of O'Connell Street'. 'Reviving' is an interesting choice. Definitions include making something popular or important again and making an improvement in someone or something's strength, condition and fortunes.

O'Connell Street has always been important but, over the last decade or so, its popularity has taken a tumble. When a young man was seriously assaulted on the street in 2019, several hundred comments online shared a common theme: the belief that O'Connell Street was a 'no-go' area. The need for change cannot be denied. And this street is not afraid of change.

Luke Gardiner was the first to see its potential, perhaps drawing similarities between Drogheda Street and his own shady origins that he preferred to keep hidden. He might have reasoned that, just like himself, the once dingy laneway only needed imagination and a sense of purpose. So, he named it after an English lord and created a sort of residential spectacle for the grandest and the wealthiest, even providing them with a sort of stage, the Mall, in which to be seen whilst taking their daily constitution.

Over time, those residents moved away and their lavish homes filled up with hotel guests, shopkeepers and all manner of businesses. Next came the fires of the Easter Rising, the War of Independence and the Civil War. Beautiful buildings might survive one fire but would be caught out on the second or third one. For instance, Drogheda House survived 1916 but was destroyed in 1922. Each rebuild involved losing something old or, at least, replacing the old with a new version of what was once there – hopefully something that felt more relevant. The Hamman Hotel, which once stood at numbers 11, 12 and 13 O'Connell Street, was also destroyed in 1922 and four years later, the Hamman Building reopened in its place for a selection of commercial tenants.

One of the key objectives of any new build is to bring back the character of this street, which will surely be done by increasing footfall, in all its variance. A busy street means less space for anti-social behaviour. With this in mind, plans are being drawn up to improve life on O'Connell Street and its surrounding area by providing a mixture of amenities – offices, hotels, a large underground metro station, restaurants, shops and apartments – that should attract an estimated six million visitors, shoppers and residents a year. Two squares, large and small, will be constructed off Henry Street, an accidental throwback to Gardiner's Mall.

But care will be taken where it can. The developers and architects have assembled a heritage team that will work diligently to achieve a balance between the old and the new. Number 42, the last surviving Georgian House from Gardiner's original street, will remain with its potential for a boutique hotel. The ten pre-1916 buildings on Moore Street will be retained, though a new walkway will be built to allow access to Moore Street when walking north on O'Connell Street, providing a nod to when

Drogheda Street was one of many streets in the region. In fact, the very fabric of the area will be monitored, from the stones used to pave the street to the parapets and roofline on O'Connell Street, whose height will not be tampered with as it is of the utmost importance to everyone that the look of the street should remain largely unchanged.

None of this will happen overnight. Indeed, a few of those mentioned are still in the initial stages of planning. Furthermore, there are the far-reaching consequences of Covid-19 to be considered. Has it changed the way we shop and will there be the usual demand for office space? When this was put to the developer's manager, he was very positive that providing attractive retail and office space will still be relevant in the years to come although, maybe, not on the same pre-Covid scale.

Meanwhile, on the west of O'Connell Street, a few doors down, Clery's will be undergoing its own revival with its exterior remaining true to the much-loved department store.

Ireland was once believed to be a backwater place, permanently out of touch with what mattered. But that was a long time ago. Over the last few years, an exciting new energy and vision has entered our culture, and our interpretation of what it is to be Irish has broadened, no matter our surname, religion, the colour of our skin or our gender. And, surely, this new era must be reflected in our capital's main street, where everyone has a right to feel at home and which is bookended by two monuments celebrating two men that devoted their careers and their very lives to effect change for the population of this island, whilst the GPO continues to commemorate those men and women who literally fought to overturn the status quo. I would like to think that every single one of them would be the first to welcome this new O'Connell Street.

Bibliography

PUBLICATIONS

Ballagh, Robert: *A Reluctant Memoir*, Head of Zeus, London, 2018.

Böll, Heinrich: *Irish Journal*, McGraw-Hill Paperbacks, NY, 1971.

Boyd, Gary A: *Dublin 1745-1922: Hospitals, Spectacle & Vice*, Four Courts Press, Dublin, 2005.

Brady, Joseph: *Dublin, 1930–1950: The Emergence of the Modern City*, Four Courts Press, Dublin, 2014.

Brady, Joseph and Simms, Anngret (eds): *Dublin Through Space and Time*, Four Courts Press, Dublin, 2001.

Bush, John: *Hibernia Curiosa: A Letter from a Gentleman in Dublin to His Friend at Dover in Kent*, J Potts & J Williams, Dublin, 1769.

Casey, Christine: *The Buildings of Ireland: Dublin*, Yale University Press, US, 2005.

Chart, David Alfred: *The Story of Dublin*, JM Dent & Co, London, 1907.

Coffey, M Thomas: *Agony at Easter, The 1916 Irish Uprising*, Penguin, London, 1969.

Corless, Damian: *From Clery's Clock to Wanderly Wagon*, The Collins Press, Cork, 2014.

Costello, Peter & Farmar, Tony: *The Very Heart of the City, The Story of Des Guiney & Clerys*, Clery & Co, Dublin, 1992.

Cullen, L M: *Eason & Son: A History*, Eason & Son Ltd, Dublin, 1989.

Cusack, Mary Francis: *The Liberator: His Life and Times*, Kenmare Publications, Kerry, 1872.

Duffy, Joe: *Just Joe, My Autobiography*, Transworld Ireland, Dublin, 2011.

Ferguson, Stephen: *The GPO: 200 Years of History*, Mercier Press, Cork, 2014.

Ferguson, Stephen: *The Post Office in Ireland*, Irish Academic Press, Kildare, 2018.

Fingall, Elizabeth, Countess of: *Seventy Years Young*, The Lilliput Press, Dublin, 1991.

Fitzgerald, Desmond: *Desmond's Rising Memoirs 1913 to Easter 1916*, Liberties Press, Dublin, 2006.

Fitz-Simon, Christopher: *The Boys, A biography of Micheál MacLíammóir and Hilton Edwards*, Heinemann, UK, 1994.

Foster, RF: Modern Ireland 1600–1972, Penguin Books, London, 1989.

Geoghegan, Professor Patrick: *Daniel O'Connell: The Man who Discovered Ireland*, Glasnevin Trust, Dublin, 1970.

Glendinning, Victoria: *Anthony Trollope*, Pimlico, London, 1988.

Gogarty, Oliver St. John: *As I Was Going Down Sackville Street*, The O'Brien Press, Dublin, 1994 (originally published 1937).

Grant, Elizabeth of Rothiemurchus: *The Highland Lady in Dublin, 1851-1856*, New Island, Dublin, 2005.

Hamilton, Sir James: *The Hamilton Manuscripts*, Archer & Sons, UK, 1869.

Hayes, Melanie: *The Best Address in Town: Henrietta Street, Dublin and Its First Residents, 1720–80*, Four Courts Press, Dublin, 2020.

Herbert, Dorothea: *Retrospections of Dorothea Herbert, 1770-1806*, TownHouse, Dublin, 2004.

Hill, Judith: *Lady Gregory: An Irish Life*, The Collins Press, Cork, 2011.

Hillier, Bevis: *John Betjeman: The Biography*, John Murray, London, 2005.

Holroyd, Michael: *Lytton Strachey: A Biography*, Penguin, London, 1980.

Kearns, Kevin C: *Dublin Voices: An Oral Folk History*, Gill & Macmillan, Dublin, 2001.

Kearns, Kevin C: *Ireland's Arctic Siege: The Big Freeze of 1947*; Gill Books, Dublin, 2011.

Kehoe, Elisabeth: *Ireland's Misfortune: The Turbulent Life of Kitty O'Shea*, Atlantic Books, London, 2009.

MacLíammóir, Micheál: *Enter a Goldfish: Memoirs of an Irish Actor, Young and Old*, Granada, London, 1981.

McCoole, Sinéad: *Hazel: A Life of Lady Lavery 1880-1935*, Lilliput Press, Dublin, 1996.

McGilligan, Patrick: *Young Orson: The Years of Luck and Genius on the Path to Citizen Kane,* Harper Perennial, NY, 2015.

McManus, Ruth: *Dublin, 1910–1940 Shaping the City & Suburbs*, Four Courts Press, Dublin, 2002.

O'Casey, Sean: *Drums Under the Windows* Macmillan & Co. Ltd, London, 1945.

O'Casey, Sean: *Pictures in the Hallway*, Macmillan & Co. Ltd, London, 1942.

O'Connor, Ulick: *The Gresham Hotel 1865–1965*, Dublin, 1965.

O'Donnell, EE: *The Annals of Dublin*, Currach Press, Dublin, 2008.

O'Donoghue, David: *Hitler's Irish Voices*, Irish Academic Press Ltd, Kildare, 2005.

Pakenham Valerie (Ed): *Maria Edgeworth's Letters from Ireland*, Lilliput Press, Dublin, 2018.

Rooney, Brendan: *Creating History, Stories of Ireland in Art*, Irish Academic Press, Kildare, 2016.

Ryan, Desmond: *The Rising: The Complete Story of Easter Week*, Golden Eagle Books, Dublin, 1966.

Shannon, Elizabeth: *Up in the Park, The Diary of the Wife of the American Ambassador to Ireland 1977-1981*, Gill and Macmillan, Dublin, 1983.

Smith, GR: *Half-a-Century in the Dead-Letter Office*, WC Hemmons, UK, 1908.

Somerville-Large, Peter: *Dublin*, Hamish Hamilton, London, 1979.

Walker, Brian M: *A Political History of the Two Irelands*, Palgrave Macmillan, London, 2012.

ARTICLES
Online resources

Catholic News Service, 'Newsfeeds 9 July 1928', https://thecatholicnewsarchive.org/crra?a=d&d=cns19280709-01.1.23.

Daly, James F, 'O'Connell Bridge and Its Environs'. *Dublin Historical Record*, Vol.14, no. 3 (1957), pp. 85-93. Old Dublin Society. http://www.jstor.org/stable/30102653.

Dublin City Council, 'O'Connell Bridge', Bridges of Dublin website, www.

bridgesofdublin.ie/bridges/oconnell-bridge/history.

Donavan, Tom, 'The Tragic Death of Constable Patrick Sheahan DMP', www.
limerickcity.ie/media/Media,4161,en.pdf, 'The Tragic Death of Constable
Patrick Sheahan DMP' by Tom Donavan

Dorney, John, 'Today in Irish History, Bloody Sunday, 21 November 1920',
www.theirishstory.com/2011/11/21/today-in-irish-history-bloody-sunday-
november-21-1920/#.X9dVRHpxfIU.

Fallon, Donal, '100 years on from the IRA assassinations of Bloody Sunday
morning, mysteries remain', *thejournal.ie*, 21 November 2020, www.thejournal.
ie/readme/bloody-sunday-1920-5272217-Nov2020.

Fennelly, Teddy, 'Flying into the History Books', *The Irish Times*, 11 April 2003,
www.irishtimes.com/culture/flying-into-the-history-books-1.355384.

Findlater, Alexander, 'Findlaters: The Story of a Dublin Merchant Family,
1774–2001', 2013, https://www.findlaters.com/chapter2.html.

Fitzgerald, Cormac, '"I was in disguise as an American tourist": The woman who
egged Richard Nixon in 1970', *thejournal.ie*, 9 June 2019, www.thejournal.ie/
richard-nixon-egged-dublin-2-4670648-Jun2019.

Fitzsimons, Eleanor, 'The Shelleys in Ireland: Passion Masquerading as Insight?',
The Keats-Shelley Review, Vol. 28, no. 1, April 2014, pp. 7–13, https://www.
tandfonline.com/doi/full/10.1179/0952414214Z.00000000037.

Fleming, Diarmaid, 'The man who blew up Nelson', *BBC News*, 12 March 2016,
https://www.bbc.com/news/magazine-35787116.

Linehan, Hugh, 'Nothing radical: The Rebuilding of Dublin', *The Irish Times*,
27 May 2016, www.irishtimes.com/culture/heritage/nothing-radical-the-
rebuilding-of-dublin-1.2663237.

Lysaght, Moira, 'Father Theobald Mathew, Apostle of Temperance'. *Dublin
Historical Record*, Vol. 36, no. 4 (1983), pp. 140–52. Old Dublin Society. http://
www.jstor.org/stable/30100738.

McNally, Frank, 'The Darling of Dublin – An Irishman's Diary about Alfie
Byrne', *The Irish Times*, 6 June 2015. www.irishtimes.com/opinion/the-darling-

of-dublin-an-irishman-s-diary-about-alfie-byrne-1.2239064.

Murphy, Pauline, 'Why Douglas Hyde, not the "Lord Mayor of Ireland", became Ireland's first President', *Irish Central*, 11 September 2018, www.irishcentral. com/roots/history/alfie-byrne-ireland-first-president.

O'Donoghue, David, 'State within a state: the Nazis in neutral Ireland', *History Ireland*. Published in 20th-century / Contemporary History, Features, Issue 6 (Nov/Dec 2006), The Emergency, Vol. 14. www.historyireland.com/20th-century-contemporary-history/state-within-a-state-the-nazis-in-neutral-ireland.

O'Dowd, Niall, 'What JFK's historic visit to Ireland in 1963 meant', *Irish Central*, 26 June 2020, www.irishcentral.com/roots/history/jfk-in-ireland.

O'Riordan, Colum, 'Cinema Building and the Strongest Woman in the World, 23 February 2017. iarc.ie/cinema-building-and-the-strongest-woman-in-the-world.

Rains, Stephanie, 'A Brief History of Clery's', *History Ireland*. Published in Issue 5 (September/October 2015), Vol. 23. www.historyireland.com/volume-23/a-brief-history-of-clerys.

Ó Riain, Micheál, 'Nelson's Pillar', *History Ireland*. Published in 18th–19th-Century History, 20th-century / Contemporary History, Features, Issue 4 (Winter 1998), Vol. 6. www.historyireland.com/20th-century-contemporary-history/nelsons-pillar.

Royal College of Physicians Ireland, 'Robert Robinson'. https://rcpi-live-cdn. s3.amazonaws.com/wp-content/uploads/2017/09/33-Robert-Robinson.pdf.

Sicker, Philip, 'Evenings at the Volta: Cinematic Afterimages in Joyce', *James Joyce Quarterly*, Vols. 42/43, nos. 1/4 (2004), pp. 99–132. University of Tulsa. http://www.jstor.org/stable/25570961.

Thorpe, Mary, 'Lillie Connolly – Mother And Rebel, Widow of James Connolly', www.historical-irishbiography.com/lillie-connolly-mother-and-rebel-widow-of-james-connolly.

Uri, John, '50 Years Ago: Apollo 13 Crew Returns Safely to Earth', Nasa Johnson Space Center website, 17 April 2020. www.nasa.gov/feature/50-years-ago-apollo-13-crew-returns-safely-to-earth.

PICTURE CREDITS

p122 Alamy; p136 © An Post/The Post Office, courtesy of the An Post Museum & Archive; pp34, 46, 53, 70, 73 (top), 86, 101, 154, 216 (top) Gareth Cheney; pp15, 57 (top), 96 Stephen Conlin; pp109, 116 Courtesy of Peter Costello Collection; p111 Courtesy of Professor James McGuire and Peter Costello; pp44, 85, 119, 160 (top), 170, 171, 179, 252 Dublin City Library and Archive; pp29, 94, 131 Flickr; p141 (top) Gillman Collection; pp90, 222-3, 231, 249 Independent News and Media; pp160, 162 Courtesy of the Irish Architectural Archive; p108 *Irish Life* Magazine; pp79, 200 ITGWU archives; p211 (KMGLM.20PO-1A35-03) Courtesy of Kilmainham Gaol Museum/OPW; p141 (bottom) Lawrence Collection/National Library of Ireland; pp32 (bottom), 63, 218 Lensmen; pp8-9, 39, 58, 149 Library of Congress; p40 Mary Evans Picture Library; p62 Lilliput Press; p210 Mercier Press Archive; p69 Museo Sveviano, Comune di Trieste; pp19, 45, 242 © National Gallery of Ireland; pp27, 32(top), 60, 78, 139 (bottom)144, 182, 192-3, 227, 240, 244 National Library of Ireland; p12 © National Monuments Service, Government of Ireland, Photographic Archive; pp57 (bottom), 76, 139 (top) Nicola Pierce; pp16, 18, 83, 103, 112, 123, 212 Peter Pearson; pp197, 233 RTÉ Archives; p73 John Sheahan; pp28, 49, 67, 95, 102, 172 Shutterstock; pp216 (bottom), 233 Derek Spiers; p203 Imogen Stuart; p117 Robert Vance; pp48, 97, 151, 152, 157, 164, 176 (both), 188, 189, 190, 204 Wiki Media; pp22, 134 Yale Center for British Art; p195 Yale University.

TEXT CREDITS

Lines from 'Jim Larkin' by Patrick Kavanagh, quoted on the Jim Larkin statue, Dublin, reprinted here by kind permission of the Trustees of the Estate of the late Katherine B Kavanagh, through the Jonathan Williams Literary Agency; Quote from *Drums Under the Windows* by Seán O'Casey, courtesy of The Estate of Sean O'Casey, MacNaughton Lord Representation; quotation from *As I Was Going Down Sackville Street* by Oliver St John Gogarty, courtesy of Colin Smythe.

Index